McMaster Journal of Theology and Ministry
ISSN 1481-0794
ISBN: 978-1-62032-688-6
Editor
Lois K. Fuller Dow

McMaster Divinity College
1280 Main Street West
Hamilton, Ontario, Canada L8S 4K1

email: mjtm@mcmaster.ca

McMaster Journal of Theology and Ministry is an electronic and print journal of McMaster Divinity College, in Hamilton, Ontario, Canada. It seeks to provide pastors, educators, and interested lay persons with the fruits of theological, biblical, and professional studies in an accessible form. It succeeds the Divinity College's former periodicals, the *Theological Bulletin*, *Theodolite*, and the *McMaster Journal of Theology*. Each volume covers an academic year (September to August). Reviews and articles are posted on the MacDiv website at:

http://www.mcmaster.ca/mjtm/

and beginning with Volume Nine (2007–2008), the volume has been available around the end of October in hard copy as well.
The *McMaster Journal of Theology and Ministry* is also available through EBSCO. Abstracts of the articles are available through Religion and Theological Abstracts.

Manuscripts, books for review, and communications should be addressed to the Editor through the email address on the journal website. Contributors are encouraged to use the style outlined in the Author Guide of Wipf and Stock, available at:

http://wipfandstock.com.
ISBN: 978-1-62032-688-6

All articles and book reviews are peer-reviewed for appropriate academic and professional standards.

Copies of the printed version can be ordered from Wipf and Stock Publishers in Eugene, Oregon, USA, 97401, and through their website, wipfandstock.com. Copies are also available at McMaster Divinity College.

Content of the *McMaster Journal of Theology and Ministry* is copyright by McMaster Divinity College.

For more information about McMaster Divinity College, please visit the College's website at www.mcmasterdivinity.info.

THE REFORMATION OF WORSHIP: A REVIEW ARTICLE

Michael Knowles
McMaster Divinity College

John Jefferson Davis. *Worship and the Reality of God: An Evangelical Theology of Real Presence*. Downers Grove, IL: IVP Academic, 2010. Pp. 231. Pbk. US$22.00. ISBN10: 0-8308-3884-8. ISBN 13: 978-0-8308-3884-4.

Michael J. Gorman. *Reading Revelation Responsibly. Uncivil Worship and Witness: Following the Lamb into the New Creation*. Eugene, OR: Cascade, 2010. Pp. xviii + 211. Pbk. US$25.00. ISBN 10: 1-60608-560-8; ISBN 13: 978-1-60608-560-8.

Ben Witherington III. *We Have Seen His Glory: A Vision of Kingdom Worship*. Calvin Institute of Christian Worship Liturgical Studies Series. Grand Rapids: Eerdmans, 2010. Pp. x + 166. Pbk. US$16.00. ISBN 10: 9780802865281. ISBN 13: 978-0802865281.

***

Concern for the renewal of congregational worship in the post-Christian West can be measured either in terms of the anxiety frequently exhibited by congregational and denominational leaders, or in relation to the continuing flood of popular and academic discussions that address this question. Three of the latter bear comparison because, intentionally or otherwise, they together reveal not only the contours of the current debate but also its unanticipated limitations.

John Jefferson Davis laments the loss of any sense of God's "real presence" in evangelical worship, a conclusion that arises from having visited 35 different worship services, representing a range of denominations and styles, in the course of a sabbatical leave. His concern is that evangelical worship focuses attention on human agents at the expense of a transcendent and holy God, and to that extent has become theologically and liturgically impoverished. This is, ultimately, less a concern for the proper conduct of evangelical worship than a call to examine the theological world view—Davis prefers to speak of "ontology"—that gives rise to proper worship. He names the alternatives that compete for our attention as scientific materialism on the one hand (with a correlative skepticism regarding miracles, the supernatural generally, and the ministry of the Holy Spirit in particular), and digital virtualism on the other (which reinforces subjectivism, elevates the role of experience, and makes the individual the arbiter of reality). In opposition to these he proposes a robust Trinitarian theism. Surveying the landscape of contemporary American evangelicalism, he calls for "a church marked by the attributes *deep, thick, different*" (32)—"deep" in terms of spirituality, "thick" in its interpersonal commitments and relationships, and distinctively "different" from mainstream American culture. According to Davis:

> The renewal of contemporary worship calls for a return to the first principles and foundations of the worship experience, beginning with an examination of the fundamental nature and essential being of the *participants* involved in worship: God, the church and the self (38; emphasis original).

Thus he appeals for a new "epistemology of faith" (54) that focuses on a God who is "heavy" (substantive, non-derivative), holy (thus awesome and numinous), joyful (rejoicing in creation, and especially in redemption), beautiful (as reflected in creation), relational (according to the foundational categories of Trinitarian theology), and available (whereby humanity is invited into the inner-divine community). The church is by consequence to be considered "high" (reflecting the transcendence of God), "heavy" (reflecting the gravity of God's purpose), and "theanthropic" (embodying the dynamics of the divine-human relationship; 60–66). In contrast to individually-focused, therapeutic, and consumerist versions of the "modern autonomous self," he views worshipers as Trinitarian (having been adopted into communion with the Holy Trinity), ecclesial (characterized by reconciliation with others), and doxological (created for worship).

Against the anti-sacramentalism and iconoclasm of the Reformation, a post-Enlightenment turn to moralism at the expense of transcendence, and an emphasis on personality and performance derived from Revivalism, Davis argues for the

> ontologically distinct nature of the space and time within which the worship-event takes place. The claim here is that, according to the theology of the New Testament, space and time themselves are altered and no longer ordinary space and ordinary time (92).

Worship, he contends, constitutes "sacred 'time travel'," in which "Sacred past and promised future are ontologically and not merely metaphorically present in the worship-event." "Similarly," he continues, "the spatial context of Sunday worship . . . is not ordinary space, but is transformed, spiritually, into sacred, kingdom space" (92–93). In practical terms, this leads Davis to advocate a "fourfold pattern of biblical worship" consisting of "gathering, ministry of the Word, ministry of the table, dismissal" (97). Notwithstanding his earlier disparagement of the digital realm, Davis invokes digital analogies, in particular virtual reality, to illustrate his argument (the communion of saints as akin to participation in the simulated "World of Warcraft" [107–10]; the Spirit as a holographic projection of Christ "into the midst of the believing church gathered around the table" [164]).

Following a lengthy historical review that cites (amongst many others) Luther, Zwingli, and Calvin, he affirms the "real presence" of Christ at the Eucharist. Intending to call the church back to a "right administration of the sacraments," Davis is optimistic that a new appropriation of traditional formularies (e.g., the *sursum corda*; "Christ has died, Christ has risen, Christ will come again") and frequent eucharistic celebration will together serve as effective means of congregational revitalization (165–66). But this thesis is subject to a simple test: if better liturgy produces better churches, then traditionally liturgical/

sacramental congregations should, on the whole, be thriving. That they are in no better shape than the constituency Davis seeks to address is, to say the least, problematic for his argument.

It is clear that, for Davis, a robust theological and historical understanding is essential to proper worship: better *understanding* makes for better worship. But this is an assumption, and not entirely consonant either with Davis's emphasis on the renewal of praxis, or with his own report of having experienced a "'glorious' . . . sense of the presence of God" in worship, the power of which he attributes not to liturgical acumen, but to intercessory prayer (197 n. 25). Furthermore, an unacknowledged conflict arises in the course of this discussion. On the one hand, Davis states unequivocally that "throughout the Bible . . . the initiative in true worship is God's" (62). In Exodus, for example,

> it is God who has "called the meeting" at his own initiative, not the people . . . God is the central actor in biblical worship, not the people; the people assemble at God's command, and they respond to his actions and directive words (98; cf. 99 n. 43).

> Modern evangelicals need to rediscover the biblical truth that in true worship it is God, not us, who is the central reality and the central actor (100).

But this sense of divine priority is difficult to reconcile with the foregoing discussion of liturgical renewal, or with explicit statements that seem to assume the opposite:

> *When* the church gathers itself together intentionally as a church, in the name of the Lord Jesus, as an assembly of God for the worship of God, *then* God himself is present, and the church can experience its full theanthropic and anthropological weight . . . (66; emphasis added).

> Christian churches need to *constitute in their practices*—especially in their practices of worship—alternative plausibility structures that can *embody and experience* the presence of the divine . . . (83; emphasis added).

A concluding chapter ("From Ontology to Doxology: From Theory to Practice in Worship Renewal") essentially recapitulates the foregoing argument in practical terms, once more affirming "the real presence of God as the central reality of every worship service" (173), reiterating the church's uniquely "theanthropic" and "charismatic" identity, and offering various practical suggestions for worship leadership. Here the term "theanthropic" bears closer scrutiny:

> The church is unique because it is, at the core of its being, in its fundamental reality, the only theanthropic ("God-bonded-to-man") reality in the universe, the likes of which never has been seen before and never will be again, a reality in which the members are bonded forever to the triune God—the gold standard of reality—in the communion of the Holy Spirit (176).

Although Davis contends that "our theanthropic union with God the Father [is] through Jesus Christ, in the communion of the Holy Spirit," surely his argument makes claims for the church that apply more properly—and uniquely—to Christ. More specifically, this proposal seems to overlook the vicarious humanity of Christ (as articulated by Athanasius and Calvin, and reiterated more recently by T. F. Torrance and Andrew Purves), a proper appreciation of which maintains the priority and unsubstitutable character of Christ's ministry on behalf of the church.[1]

This theological distinction points to an unresolved tension that underlies the book as a whole (and much of evangelical worship as well): why, if the church is by nature "high, heavy, and theanthropic," does its worship so often fail to express this truth? Conversely, if this is antecedently the church's true character, in what way might adjustments to worship *practice* serve to effect congregational renewal? Stated differently, while Davis properly insists that "in true worship it is God, not us, who is the central reality and the central actor" (100), much of his argument focuses instead on human agency. A clearer resolution

---

1. See, for example, Andrew Purves, *Reconstructing Pastoral Theology: A Christological Foundation*. Louisville: Westminster John Knox, 2004, 47–77.

to the basic question of "who does what" is, surely, critical to any rediscovery of biblical worship. Still, Davis is by no means alone in being unable to solve this impasse.

Not unlike those of Davis, Ben Witherington's observations on worship were occasioned by two considerations: the absence of any comprehensive treatment of the subject by other biblical scholars, and the experience of pastoring six churches in the course of a thirty-year academic career.

He begins with an exposition of the conversation between Jesus and the Samaritan woman in John 4, concluding that "Jesus is inaugurating a worship without temples, priests and literal sacrifices, all of which are said to be fulfilled by and in Jesus" (8). Next comes an exposition of Revelation 4 and 5, much of which reproduces the text of a lengthy sermon (13–20). Here Witherington observes, "The chief aim of worship is that we be caught up in wonder, love, and praise of God, and thereby get a glimpse of the heavenly worship which happens when and as we are worshipping" (19). How this should transpire is less clear: again, such worship is apparently initiated by God (21), yet according to Witherington, John of the Apocalypse likely prepared himself beforehand to receive the heavenly vision ("he had already immersed himself in the divine presence before the vision came . . . he had prepared his heart to worship, he had repented of his sins . . . and so he boldly approached the Presence," 17), and therefore so must we. In the ensuing treatment of 2 Cor 3:18, Witherington proposes that while it is God who transforms the worshipper, "Adoration is the means of our glorification. Glorifying God is the means of our transformation into Christ's image" (25). Likewise in the discussion of Rom 12:2 ("do not be conformed . . . but be transformed"), the key verbs are said to refer "to a constant and ongoing process that requires one to work at de-enculturating oneself and re-orienting oneself" (37–38). Yet this assertion ignores the theological implications of the passive voice in both verbs. In each case the implication seems to be that proper conduct on the part of the church is essential to true worship; indeed that worship, rightly performed, creates the vision of which it speaks.

If this is the case then, as Davis also argues, improvements to the conduct of worship might be expected to improve the congregants' experience of worship. As previously, however, such a proposal raises difficult theological issues: particularly in light of Christology, in what way does worship constitute a theological vision when worship itself is ostensibly a response to that vision?

Witherington deals at some length with questions of Jewish influence on the worship of the early church: theological discontinuity, in that Jewish worship is oriented to rest and Sabbath, whereas Christian worship looks forward to the fulfillment of the new creation (Chapter 3); continuity in the adoption from synagogal practice of structured worship, hierarchical leadership structures, and the use of purpose-built edifices (Chapter 4). Next comes an exposition of Eph 5:18–20 and Col 3:16–17 ("psalms, hymns, and spiritual songs"): "What these verses suggest is both old and new elements in Christian worship when it came to music" (66). This leads to discussion of doxological fragments embedded in the New Testament (Phil 2:6–11, Jude 24–25, Heb 13:20–21) and an extended exposition of the Lord's Prayer (according to Matthew) in relation to chapter 10 of the *Didache* (68–84).

Chapter 6, "Illuminating the Good News," addresses "The Oral and Rhetorical World of the Apostles." The chapter begins with an introduction to and defense of rhetorical analysis of New Testament letters as documents intended for oral performance (with a corollary dismissal of epistolary analysis). Next comes lengthy discussion of "The Preaching of Early Christian Orators" (Hebrews as alternating between *synkresis* and paraenesis; First John as "epideictic rhetoric"; James as diatribe and enthymematic argumentation; First Corinthians as "deliberative discourse"; 98–122). The relevance of this section to an understanding of worship as an activity in its own right, whether ancient or modern, is unclear at best. The same observation applies to the treatment of Paul's refusal to accept remuneration from the Corinthian church (123–26). As the footnotes indicate, much of this material appears to represent a condensation of discussions that the author has published in fuller form elsewhere. To this point, one gets the impression of a series of notes and observations only loosely organized under the heading of "worship," but lacking a single, consistently argued thesis.

The last two chapters are perhaps the strongest section of the book, as they come closer to articulating the theological vision that, for Witherington, underlies Christian worship. As he observes in relation to Col 2:20–23:

> I submit that Christian worship should be living out of the new realities, the new life we have in Christ, the new focus on the heavenly Christ who will one day return, and not focussing on anything earthly: the old earthly forms of worship, the old ascetical practices, the old ethnic, social, and secular distinctions . . . In short, all actions should be doxological (135–36).

This is followed by sensitive and thoughtful discussions of the place of work (and Sabbath) in relation to prayer and worship within the new creation inaugurated by Christ (139–40), and of Paul's ethic of mutual responsibility (2 Thess 3:6–13; Gal 6:2–6) within the community of faith. Chapter 8 ("Doxology: The End and Aim of All Things") continues to draw together the diverse strands of the foregoing discussion, emphasizing the priority of theological substance over style (154), with particular attention to doxology ("The focus must be on God and the glory must be given to God," 154) and Christology ("Christian worship should most often have a Christocentric focus," 155).

At this point, however, the same critical tension between human and divine agency emerges once more: "The Bible says that without vision the people perish, and this is especially true without a vision of proper worship, for *worship is the means God uses to mold us into our better selves*" (150; emphasis original). If that is indeed the case, surely John Jefferson Davis has nothing to complain about: faithful worship should, of necessity, successfully invoke the reality of which it speaks. Conversely, if Davis's complaints are valid, Witherington needs to account more fully for his assertion, and provide an explanation of how such transformation actually takes place. Although its title promises *A Vision of Kingdom Worship*, perhaps it would be fairer to say that this book for the most part describes selected components of first-century Christian worship *practice*, without, however, adequately exploring the actual vision that gave (and gives) rise to such worship, or makes worship possible in the face of human inadequacy. For that we must turn to the worship of John on Patmos.

In many ways the most helpful of the three studies is Michael Gorman's treatment of the book of Revelation, which is unexpected because explaining worship is only one aspect of the author's broader exegetical purpose. Yet in the course of exposition Gorman manages to describe the inner dynamic of worship, attending less to matters of "when," "where," and "how" (the primary focus of the previous two works) than to the more central question of "why": "As a prophetic summons to first-commandment faithfulness, Revelation is both a call to worship the true God and a call to forsake all false deities" (34). Worship, Gorman affirms, is essentially a political gesture, a public declaration of one's allegiance and orientation to that which is theologically (and therefore also socially, politically, and culturally) absolute. The difference in this case is that the Book of Revelation is explicit about the vision—or visions—that impel worship, and the distinctive gestures to which different visions give rise.

Where Gorman ventures next will occasion a sharp intake of breath on the part of at least some readers, for we are treated to an extended, carefully nuanced discussion both of Roman imperial theology (including worship of the emperor) and—in painful detail—of American civil religion. This juxtaposition provides the context for Gorman's main thesis: "*Revelation is a manifesto against civil religion and a summons to uncivil worship and witness*" (55). Such analyses are not new, but what makes Gorman's treatment striking is his intentional address to that segment of the American church which—ironically—values the Book of Revelation most highly:

> I would contend, in fact, that the most alluring and dangerous deity in the United States is the omnipresent, syncretistic god of nationalism mixed with Christianity lite: religious beliefs, language, and practices that are superficially Christian but infused with national myths and habits. Sadly, most of this civil religion's practitioners belong to

Christian churches, which is precisely why Revelation is addressed to the seven *churches* (not to Babylon), to all Christians tempted by the civil cult (56).

Such an approach will not endear the book to its intended audience, any more than will Gorman's extended critique of the "Left Behind" series (and its take on Revelation) in the following chapter, or his deconstruction of historical dispensationalism.

More positively, Gorman's particular contribution is to expound the proper rationale for authentic worship, which is a renewed vision of God such as that which John experienced on the island of Patmos: "Revelation provides this vision of 'uncivil' worship . . . centered on the throne of the eternal holy God and the faithful slaughtered Lamb, and on the coming new creation" (76). Accordingly, Gorman identifies the throne room scene in Revelation 4–5 as the theological anchor and "hermeneutical . . . key" (103) for the book of Revelation as a whole. Worship, in this view (and not just the worship depicted within the book itself), begins with a vision of the Lamb who was slain, and his redemption of creation by means of paradoxical "power in weakness," thereby revealing the true character and purpose of God. For readers familiar with Gorman's approach to Paul (especially *Cruciformity: Paul's Narrative Spirituality of the Cross* [Eerdmans, 2001] and *Inhabiting the Cruciform God: Kenosis, Justification, and Theosis in Paul's Narrative Soteriology* [Eerdmans, 2009]), this interpretation will come as no surprise. But such an approach is especially relevant in the case of Revelation, both because of the powerlessness of its original recipients and (more pertinently) because of a tendency on the part of some to read the book today in a manner that buttresses their own theologies of "coercive divine power" (111).

This is not to say that Gorman has an obvious political or theological axe to grind: he is content, rather, simply to sketch out the essential plot contours and key players in the eschatological drama. Here a central theological dynamic of Revelation is the contrast between true and false worship: between the demonic powers and human institutions that claim ultimate allegiance, and God who alone is worthy of it. "Faithful witness" in this context is thus a matter of faithful, rightly oriented worship, whether or not it succeeds in persuading others to follow suit (132). Rather than inveighing against contemporary evils, however, Gorman to this point maintains a light touch, identifying areas where the book of Revelation should inspire more careful theological reflection. Foremost among the latter are the question of whether followers of the slain Lamb may serve in the military, and how Christian economic practice can "promote justice and the healing of the nations" (149).

As might be expected, much of the discussion focuses on the problematic issue of divine judgment, and of the role of the saints in its execution. Here Gorman affirms that the saints' cry for justice (Rev 6:9–11; 19:1–4) is itself an expression of worship, which celebrates the righteous agency of God rather than seeking retribution or taking up arms: "The church celebrates the victory it has longed for only because the judgment of Babylon means the salvation of the world" (158). Likewise the vision of a harmonious human community—the "New Jerusalem"—with which Revelation concludes is implicitly liturgical. From this perspective worship is less an activity to be conducted at a particular time or place, or in a particular manner, than it is an integral aspect of life in the presence of God: there is no temple in the city because "its temple is the Lord God the Almighty and the Lamb" (Rev 21:22; so pp. 163, 166–67).

In the last analysis, worship is a function of spirituality, the focus of Gorman's concluding chapter. Indeed, "worship" heads a list of seven topics that he discusses in summarizing the "performative or narrative spirituality" (178) inculcated by this book. Here Gorman's critique of civil religion becomes more pointed, as he urges the church to abandon its customary celebration of "syncretistic patriotism" in favor of faithful testimony to the suffering and triumphant Lamb:

> That this self-evident truth about worship seems so odd, so radical, simply demonstrates how comfortable the church has become in bed with the beast.

The choice between the two, Gorman insists, "*is an either-or proposition with very serious consequences*" (179–80; emphasis original). From this point proceed discussions of spiritual discernment, prophetic resistance, self-criticism, non-violent speech and action, communal witness, and hope.

As contemporary evangelicals (and others) search for a new sense of worship, a comparison of these three studies indicates how much easier it is to focus on particular forms of worship, or to urge more faithful practice in hope of effecting congregational change. This is not to disparage such approaches, which have much to offer by way of practical advice. But in the last analysis, for the church to escape the dual dangers of formalism and Pelagianism that currently mute and numb so much of its testimony will require a more bracing challenge of the sort that Gorman offers, a true re-visioning of our worship that focuses on the One who not only deserves but inspires it. My guess is that *Reading Revelation Responsibly* will be dismissed as "un-Christian" by those who most need to hear it. Yet of the three it makes by far the most trenchant observations on the nature of worship, and has the most to offer towards the renewal of worship in the church today.

In hindsight, might it be that attention to performance and participation, proper leadership and appropriate form, are the problem rather than the solution to much of what ails evangelical worship today? In a manner that is difficult to distinguish from the broader tendencies of Western culture, the church seems profoundly addicted to performance and spectacle, to the creation of "meaningful experiences" for the benefit of participants. But might it be, in fact, that God resists our attempts at making him relevant, and that "consumer satisfaction" (however carefully construed) is ultimately incompatible with true worship? Against all expectation, it is the vision of a suffering exile, one seemingly least able to effect change in the church of his day, that offers the most sobering and salutary insights into the nature of worship and the possibility of its renewal today.

THE PROBLEM OF EVIL

James P. Danaher
Nyack College, Nyack, NY

What theologians refer to as "the problem of evil" results from the fact that if God is all-good, all-knowing, all-powerful, and the sole creator of the universe, how do we explain the existence of evil? This creates what logicians call inconsistency. We can resolve the inconsistency by removing any one of the above-mentioned attributes of God. If God were not all-good there would obviously be evil in the world because of the evil in the creator. Likewise, if God were not all-knowing, he could have created a world that he thought would be free of evil without knowing that evil would result from his creation. We could even understand God to be less than all-powerful, or we could imagine that God was not the sole creator of the universe. Any one of these options would explain the presence of evil.

Most Christians, however, have been reluctant to resolve this inconsistency by denying any one of these divine attributes. Instead, some have attempted to show that there is something wrong with our concept of evil.[1] Things may appear evil to us but that is to perceive things from our limited perspective; it is to view things in light of what we like or do not like. If we could see things from God's eternal perspective, we would see them very differently. Unfortunately, the result of such a position is that it tends to make us less than compassionate. When people are suffering, if we believe that the evil they suffer is only apparent and not ultimately real, we will tend to lack the very important virtue of compassion. Jesus extended true compassion to people who suffered the evil of this world, and he calls us to do the same. A diminished capacity for compassion is a high price to pay for exonerating God as the cause of evil.

1. Danaher, *Eyes That See*, 75–77.

Over the centuries, philosophers and theologians have proposed a host of other possible ways to explain or justify the existence of evil. Most compelling for me is the idea of evil as instrumental. Philosopher John Hick has written extensively on the idea of evil as a necessary ingredient in God's purpose of making us into his likeness.[2] Hick claims that God has made us in his image and likeness,[3] but although we bear the image of God from birth, the likeness of God takes a lifetime to develop. In that process, God uses what we call evil as an instrument to that purpose. Just as a medical operation might be painful and undesirable in itself, it can have the consequence of restoring us to health. Likewise, God uses what we consider evil to make us into his likeness.

Hick, like many people, thinks that God's perfecting of us and making us into his likeness is largely a matter of perfecting our moral behavior. The perfection that Jesus calls us to, however, is not about becoming like him in terms of being sinless but in terms of becoming his agents of forgiveness and mercy. Interestingly, if we find our perfection in our becoming forgiving rather than sinless, the existence of evil is very consistent with an all-good, all-knowing, and all-powerful sole creator. If what it means to follow Jesus is much more a matter of becoming agents of God's forgiveness and mercy, it makes sense that God would create a world that would give us the greatest possible opportunity to develop those divine attributes. If we are to become loving as God is loving and we extend our love to sinners and even our enemies[4] through forgiveness and mercy, it makes sense that God would create a world full of sinners and enemies in order to give us the greatest possible opportunity to develop into his forgiving likeness.

Of course, we do not want a God whose purpose for our lives is to transform us into people who can love sinners and enemies.

---

2. Hick, *Evil*.
3. Gen 1:26.
4. Jesus washes the feet of Judas (John 13:2–5), and prays from the cross for his torturers to be forgiven in order that they might spend eternity with him (Luke 23:34).

We want God to be a moral cop, who enforces divine justice, which we imagine is a matter of rewarding good behavior and punishing bad behavior. We want God to be the enforcer of the kind of order we would want if we were God. If we were God, we would base our sovereignty upon power and reward those who obey us and punish those who dare to disobey. The God that Jesus reveals, however, bases his sovereignty upon forgiveness and love. The Jesus revelation is that of a loving God who desires to produce love within his creation. His great purpose behind creation is to create people who, like himself, are able to change others, not through the threat of force, but through forgiveness and love. In order to accomplish that purpose, we must participate by becoming ever more aware of the forgiveness he constantly extends to us.

Jesus tells us that "The one to whom little is forgiven, loves little."[5] Conversely, to love much, we must experience much forgiveness. We usually understand this to mean that the one with the greater sin and therefore greater forgiveness will love more, but that is a wrong way to understand the idea of receiving much forgiveness. We are forgetful creatures and no matter how great our offense might be, in no time we forget its graveness and the grandness of the forgiveness we received. In fact, Jesus tells a story to illustrate this fact. He tells us of an unforgiving servant who, after his master has forgiven him a great deal, does not forgive another who owes him a very small amount.[6] Like all of Jesus' parables, this is not telling us about a particular unappreciative individual. Jesus is instead relating a universal truth that applies to almost all of us. We are all forgetful that others have forgiven us, and are acutely aware of the offenses we have suffered. The only way to reverse this process is to experience forgiveness on an almost constant basis. By constantly being aware of receiving forgiveness, we do, in time, become more forgiving ourselves and respond to others with forgiveness rather than a demand for justice. Thus, the one who habitually receives forgiveness is more likely to become forgiving than the one who

---

5. Luke 7:47. Scripture quotations are from the NRSV.
6. Matt 18:23–35.

experiences a single, great act of forgiveness that easily slips from memory.

This is the great problem with imagining that God forgives us in one act of atonement for all time, and never again suffers the offense of our sin. If Jesus suffered the offense of our sin, once and for all, then we have no continual need of repentance, and likewise no continual source from which to experience God's forgiveness. The truth is that God continues to suffer our rejection of him, and we continually need to repent and experience his forgiveness for our failure to love God the way that Jesus calls us to love him with our whole heart, soul, mind, and strength.

In order to understand this, we must see that our sin is much deeper than we imagine, and we grieve the heart of God long before any evil behavior appears. Likewise, God's desire is that we would repent long before any evil or destructive behavior appears; that is, that we would repent or turn back to an awareness of God's presence every time we find ourselves distracted from an awareness of his presence. God's desire is that we would all live the way Jesus lived; that is, in a constant awareness of the Father's presence. Whenever we leave such a state of prayer we need to turn back or repent. Our culture may imagine that the sins that separate us from God are things like murder or adultery, but Jesus was sinless not just because he avoided such behaviors, but because he was never distracted from an awareness of his Father's presence. Throughout the Gospels, Jesus offers many teachings in order to reveal sins that our culture finds difficult to see as sinful. In the story of the Great Banquet,[7] the reason that people chose not to come to the feast was not that they chose instead to be at a crack house or bordello, but because they were doing business or getting married. We assume there is nothing wrong with doing business or getting married, but Jesus tells us that anything that keeps us from God's great banquet is cause for repentance. Indeed, we are almost all kept from the fullness of life that God has for us by innocuous activities that occupy us in ways that keep us from an awareness of God's presence.

---

7. Luke 14:16–24.

Jesus is constantly pointing out that the standard to which God is calling us is much greater than we would like to imagine, and that there is a judgment. The judgment is that we have all failed to live the fullness of life that God intends for us. The intention of judgment, however, is to bring us to repentance so that we may experience God's forgiveness. We have all gone our own way and sought to find life and meaning apart from God. Our hearts are prone to wander, but it is the recognition of that sin that causes us to return to an awareness of God's presence through repentance, and the experience of God's forgiveness.

At this point, we should better understand why an all-good and all-powerful creator would fashion a world where human beings would constantly be tempted to go off on their own to seek life and meaning apart from God. It is only in a world where the opportunity for sin and all the subsequent evil is abundant, that there is equally the opportunity to come to know the greatness of God's forgiveness and mercy. Such a world provides countless opportunities to both receive forgiveness from God and to practice our divine likeness by extending it to others.

We may find it strange that God would create a world so ripe with evil, but that is because we equate evil with pain and suffering, the absence of which we consider happiness. Jesus, however, points to a deeper, richer, and more divine happiness. The happiness he has for us draws us into the pain and suffering that is so much a part of forgiveness and love. We find this hard to understand. We want God to be who we would be if we were God. If we were God, we would destroy those portions of creation that did not immediately conform to our idea of what is good. We would punish the prodigal son while rewarding the good son.[8] We, like Jonah, would have God punish evil and eliminate those people who are unlike us in their morality or theology. We understand neither God's love, nor his ultimate purpose behind creation, and therefore we do not understand his tolerance of evil. True, there are places in Scripture where God does seem to sanction violence in order to eliminate evil, but his desire is always to transform evil through forgiveness. Henri

---

8. Luke 15:11–32.

Nouwen puts it best. If evil is seen only as an irreversible, clearly visible, and sharply outlined tumor, then there is only one possibility: cut it out. Here, violence is necessary. But when evil is reversible and can be turned into good through forgiveness, then nonviolence becomes possible.[9]

God's desire is always for transformation through forgiveness, and it is for that reason that God is so tolerant of evil. Indeed, God tolerates evil and is "kind to the ungrateful and the wicked,"[10] not simply because they are his creation—his beloved sons and daughters—but because God knows that the ungrateful and the wicked might be the very ones with the greatest potential to realize God's ultimate purpose. That is, they may have the greatest potential to become the forgiving and merciful likeness of Jesus. God knows that often the greatest sinner makes the greatest saint, and that we ultimately come to know who God is not by doing it right but by doing it wrong. We see many examples of this throughout Scripture: Moses, David, and Paul are murderers or accomplices to murder, and yet God uses them because they come to know God in a way that most of us never do. Likewise, in the genealogy of Jesus, of the five women mentioned, one is an adulteress, one a prostitute, and another pretends to be a prostitute in order to get pregnant from her own father-in-law. There is something about doing it wrong that makes us understand God's heart in a way that we never understand by doing it right. The father in the story of the prodigal loves the good, older son as much as the prodigal, but the prodigal comes to comprehend the father's love in a way that the good, older son never does.

In that same fifteenth chapter of Luke's Gospel, where Jesus tells the story of the Prodigal Son, he tells another parable about the Lost Sheep. At the end of that parable Jesus says, "I tell you that in the same way there will be more rejoicing in heaven over one sinner who repents than over ninety-nine righteous persons who do not need to repent."[11] If the Gospel were about doing it

---

9. Nouwen, *Encounters*, 102.
10. Luke 6:35.
11. Luke 15:7.

right, why would there be more rejoicing over someone that did it wrong rather than those that do it right and have no need of repentance? What is so wonderful about repentance that there is rejoicing in heaven? There are probably many reasons for the rejoicing in heaven over the repentant sinner, but one is that only the repentant sinner knows who God is. We discover the truth of God's divine, forgiving nature only through repentance, and the experience of his forgiveness.

Of course, this does not mean that we should indulge in sinful behavior in order to experience God's forgiveness. That is not necessary since our sin occurs, and we grieve the heart of God, long before any evil behavior appears; we are ripe with opportunities for repentance and the experience of God's forgiveness. Likewise, we should not take all this talk to mean that we are not to oppose evil. Evil is to be opposed, but our opposition to evil should always be with compassion. Evil should always be opposed with the kind of compassion that will lead to repentance and the experience of God's forgiveness. The hope and purpose of our confrontation of evil, whether in others or ourselves, should always be intent upon bringing about the experience of God's forgiveness in order that we might be changed into his likeness. In order to do that, we must oppose evil and the suffering it produces in a very different way than that to which human beings have become accustomed. Jesus does not come into the world to destroy evil and suffering, but to show us how we can transform evil and suffering and therein be made ever more into God's forgiving and loving likeness.

The real key to understanding the problem of evil is to understand the incarnation. God not only created a world that abounds in evil and suffering, but he entered into that world in order to show us how to become like him in terms of forgiveness and love. This is the great mystery of incarnation. Some atonement theories have tried to end that mystery and explain atonement as a matter of God punishing Jesus for our sin, but the revelation of Jesus on the cross is the revelation of a God who transforms evil by suffering it and releasing it through forgiveness. This is the divine revelation of the cross; and those that have taken it seriously and have followed Jesus to their own crosses by suffering evil and releasing it through forgiveness, have found themselves become a little more like God.

There is something so divinely beautiful about God entering into the suffering of the world that it confounds our understanding, but although our understanding may not comprehend it, we can experience it ourselves by entering into the suffering of others. Think of the person you love most in this world and recall those times when you felt closest to them—when you felt that closeness that goes beyond what we normally feel as human beings. They were almost always times of suffering. Nothing brings us together like suffering. Great suffering and great love are the things that transform us, and they are often experienced together.

Sadly, this is not the message we all too often hear from religious people. Instead we are told that religious righteousness is about confronting evil with violence and eliminating it rather than transforming it and letting it transform us. What we hear from most religious people is that God hates evil and the suffering it causes, and obedient followers of God should do everything in their power to eliminate it. What is behind such thinking is the idea of holiness as sinlessness. That was certainly the Pharisees notion of holiness, but Jesus tells us that holiness is very different from what the Pharisees imagined. Jesus' notion of being holy, as God is holy, is not a matter of being sinless, but a matter of being merciful and forgiving as God is merciful and forgiving. That kind of holiness only comes through an ever-greater experience of God's mercy and forgiveness. Such experience is not the result of increased sin in our lives but an increased awareness of the depth of our sin.

There have always been these two very different notions of holiness. Unfortunately, the pharisaic notion of holiness as sinlessness is the more common among religious people, while the kind of holiness of which Jesus speaks is rarer. Rare as it may be, however, we can still see that kind of holiness in those individuals who are conscious of the depth of their sin, and consequently live in an almost constant state of repentance and the experience of God's mercy and forgiveness. These are God's agents of the mercy and forgiveness by which the world continues to be transformed.

Bibliography

Danaher, James P. *Eyes That See, Ears That Hear: Perceiving Jesus in a Postmodern Context.* Liguori, MO: Liguori, 2006.

Hick, John. *Evil and the God of Love.* Rev. ed. New York: Harper & Row, 1977.

Nouwen, Henri. *Encounters with Merton.* New York: Crossroad, 1981.

Forgiveness and Reconciliation in Old Testament Sacrifice

Anna Suk Yee Lee
McMaster Divinity College

Introduction

The twenty-first century has begun with social disintegration and human estrangement. Broken relationships are experienced everywhere. There are urgent cries for the cessation of hostilities and the advent of peace. The restoration of a good relationship between hostile parties can only be rooted in true forgiveness and reconciliation. For Christians, the teachings on forgiveness and reconciliation in the Scriptures offer crucial guidance in response to this situation. The Old Testament provides rich illumination on this topic, especially in the sacrificial legislation in the book of Leviticus. Through the Old Testament sacrificial system, God promised to forgive and be reconciled with repentant worshippers, thus enabling them to draw near to the Lord again. Nevertheless, it is important to ask how the sacrificial system worked and in what conditions the forgiveness was granted and reconciliation became effectual.

In this paper, we will investigate the purification and reparation offerings in Leviticus in order to articulate the theological truth and implications of forgiveness and reconciliation. I aim at demonstrating the hallmarks of genuine forgiveness and reconciliation embedded in the Old Testament sacrificial rituals.

Expiatory Sacrifices in Leviticus

The book of Leviticus is God's revelation to his newly established people at the tent of meeting that was erected at Sinai (Lev

27:34). The purpose of this revelation is to ensure the enduring presence of Yahweh within the community and to nurture the covenant relationship established with him.¹

Leviticus begins with the gifts of sacrifice, which is the heart of public worship.² Chapters 1–7 outline the five major offerings: burnt offering, cereal offering, well-being offering, purification offering, and reparation offering. The first three are voluntary gifts characterized by the phrase "a soothing aroma to the Lord" (ריח־ניחוח ליהוה Lev 1:9; cf. 1:13, 17; 2:2, 9; 3:5), and function as expressions of praise and homage to God (Leviticus 1–3).³ The last two sacrifices are required because of sin, reflecting notions of atonement, forgiveness, and restitution.⁴ They function as channels of the Lord for sinners to express their penitence and to plead for divine forgiveness.

The purification offering (חטאת; Lev 4:1–5:13)⁵ and reparation offering (אשם; Lev 5:14–6:7 [MT: 5:14–26])⁶ are expiatory gifts that deal with sin that disrupts the relationship with God and his created world.⁷ These remedial offerings attend to unintentional sins only. By contrast, Num 15:30–31 states that intentional sins cannot be expiated.⁸ Both offerings, presided

---

1. Boda, *A Severe Mercy*, 55.
2. Gane, *Leviticus, Numbers*, 57.
3. Boda, *A Severe Mercy*, 66.
4. Budd, *Leviticus*, 77. These offerings and concepts will be discussed in detail below.
5. Nearly all versions and translations render חטאת as "sin offering." However, Milgrom argues successfully that this term would be better understood as referring to the process of purification, especially since חטאת sometimes is used in situations that have no relation to sin, such as Leviticus 12, where the blood acts as the purging agent. In this paper, חטאת is translated as "purification offering" in accordance with Milgrom's suggestion (Milgrom, *Studies in Cultic Theology*, 67–69).
6. Most of the versions render אשם as "guilt offering." According to the nature of the sacrifice, Milgrom suggests that this term should be translated as "reparation offering," which is adopted in this paper (Milgrom, *Cult and Conscience*, 3–12).
7. Expiatory gift refers to the compensation for the wrongdoing.
8. Milgrom argues that confession, which only appears in four priestly passages (Lev 5:5; 16:21; 26:40; Num 5:6–7), "is the legal device fashioned by the priestly legislators to convert deliberate sins into inadvertences, thereby

over by the priest, are presented publicly in the tent of meeting before the Lord (לפני יהוה), the one who receives the sacrificial gifts (Lev 4:4; cf. 4:15, 24, 31; 5:6, 7, 12, 19; 6:7 [MT: 5:26]). This setting implies that sins, even when committed by an individual, are not private affairs. The remedy for sin must be made before the Lord, as all sins are sins against God (the offended), thus threatening his holy presence and endangering the solidarity of the whole community (cf. Ps 51:4 [MT: 51:6]).[9]

The reparation offering, which operates similarly to the purification offering, not only provides expiation for sin, especially an unfaithful act (תמעל מעל; Lev 5:15; cf. 6:2 [MT: 5:21]), but also serves as a means of reparation. The use of the verb השיב (restore) in parallel with שלם (restitution) suggests a legal context in which the offender has to compensate for the loss in full and add one-fifth more as a penalty (Lev 5:6; 6:4–5 [MT: 5:23–24]). The guilty parties have to give the total sum to those who have suffered the damages before they can present their reparation offerings to the Lord (Lev 6:5–6 [MT: 5:24–25]). This is the only sacrifice that can be converted into money (Lev 5:15, 18; 6:6 [MT: 5:25]), thus facilitating payment.[10] This unique step demonstrates that forgiveness from God cannot be secured until rectification has been made with the one who has been harmed.

Ritual achieves its goal through a process of activities,[11] which, according to Gilders, is a mode of communication that is

---

qualifying them for sacrificial expiation." See the case of intentional sin in Lev 5:1 (Milgrom, *Leviticus 1–16*, 301–2). Boda disagrees with Milgrom's proposal and suggests that sins should be divided into three types categorized according to intent: "inadvertent errors that can be forgiven/purified, deliberate errors that can be forgiven, and defiant sin that cannot be forgiven" (Boda, *A Severe Mercy*, 60; cf. Kiuchi, *Leviticus*, 59–60).

9. Boda, *A Severe Mercy*, 60; Kiuchi, *Leviticus*, 107.

10. The reparation offering in the priestly system is the most difficult to understand and its distinction from a purification offering, as Milgrom states, "has been the despair of scholars through the ages" (Milgrom, *Cult and Conscience*, 1, 14). See Anderson, "Sacrifice and Sacrificial Offerings," 880.

11. Gane states that a ritual is an activity system with meaning attached to its physical activities. The goal for such a system is to accomplish a particular "transformation" through an activity process. He stipulates that it is not the activities that define the system but the "goal" of the ritual that determines

accomplished through symbols attached to the activities.[12] Thus, examining the sacrificial process is important for an understanding of the goal of the expiatory offering. The ritual procedure varies for four classes of offenders: the anointed priest, the whole congregation, a ruler, and a common person.[13] The variation is primarily based on the impact of the sin on the community as a whole.[14] Except when fine flour is the offering, the atonement process generally involves the following five steps:

By the offender:

(1) Compensate the loss of the injured party (for reparation offerings only).

(2) Bring an unblemished animal to the tent of meeting.

(3) Lay a hand on the animal so as to identify oneself with the animal, which one then slays.

By the priest:

(4) Perform the blood ritual and handle the animal remains to signify the removal of impurity.

By the Lord:

(5) A forgiveness formula is proclaimed: "so the priest shall make atonement for them, and they will be forgiven" (וכפר עלהם הכהן ונסלח להם:; Lev 4:20; cf. 4:26, 31, 35; 5:10, 13, 18; 6:7 [MT: 5:26]) to imply the granting of forgiveness.[15]

---

which activities are necessary to achieve the desired change. Therefore, the goal of the expiatory offering defines the activities that should be included and the way they should be performed. Understanding this will aid in the interpretation of the ritual in Leviticus. See Gane, *Cult Character*, 3–24.

12. Gilders, *Blood Ritual*, 3. Douglas also urges against imposing the Deuteronomic version on the Levitical one, as Leviticus's literary style works through analogies (Douglas, *Leviticus as Literature*, 13, 18).

13. This procedure, although referring to the purification offering, should be shared by both purification and reparatory offerings.

14. The economic means of the individual offerer were also considered (Lev 4:27–35).

15. This formula is only absent in the purification offering of the anointed priest. The reason is not stated explicitly and scholars have differing opinions. Kiuchi suggests that the anointed priest is not forgiven as the ritual is not sufficient to atone for him (Kiuchi, *Leviticus*, 95). Perhaps this is why the anointed priest needs to make atonement for himself and his household before carrying out any other rituals during the Day of Atonement (Lev 16:11).

The structure of the process above reveals that expiatory sacrifice is a somber offering, with forgiveness as its objective. This complicated procedure is a reminder that the offender needs to take remedial measures before forgiveness is granted. First, the offender still suffers loss as the sacrifice is costly. Second, the laying on of the hand and the slaying of the animal in the worship center implies that the offerer must admit and confess their sin publicly.[16] Third, the extra step in the reparation offering reveals that the offender, besides rectifying the relationship with God, must also compensate the damage caused to other parties. Finally, with the assistance of the priest who performs the blood ritual, forgiveness from God will be granted. As a result, the offerer can be reconciled to both God and the world.[17] If the purification offering focuses on vertical forgiveness, the reparation offering pulls in the dimension of horizontal forgiveness. Both dimensions are important in the expiatory sacrifice.

Sin and Consequence

The purpose of expiatory sacrifice is remedial, that is, to address the negative consequence of sin.[18] The priestly literature stresses that sin will incur punitive judgment from the Divine, who is the offended party whenever a human sins.[19] This punishment is

---

However, Milgrom argues that the formula that appears in Lev 4:20 should also cover the anointed priest, as the purification offerings of the anointed priest and the whole congregation should be viewed as a single case running from Lev 4:1 to Lev 4:21 (Milgrom, *Leviticus 1–16*, 241).

16. Although the word "confess" (וְהִתְוַדָּה) only appears in 5:5 within Lev 4:1–6:7. However, confession can be implied through the actions performed by the offender during the sacrificial process in the public worship center.

17. Balentine, *Leviticus*, 50; Milgrom, *Leviticus 1–16*, 370.

18. For detailed discussion about sin and consequence, see Sklar's work (Sklar, *Sin, Impurity, Sacrifice, Atonement*, 11–43).

19. See the discussion above regarding God as the offended party in the context of human sin. The negative consequence that follows sin might be due to divine retribution (either executed directly by the Lord or by the covenant community on his behalf) or natural consequences not resulting from an external judgment of the Lord who may be involved in the process but not in a

either executed by the Lord himself (e.g., Lev 10:1–2) or by the faith community (e.g., Lev 20:2–5), who should respond eagerly as sin threatens God's presence within the community and endangers the community's survival.

The connection between sin and punishment is so strong that, in the Old Testament, the terms "sin" (חטא) or "guilt" (אשם) can refer, according to context, to the wrong itself or to the penalties of the wrong (e.g., Zech 14:18–19). The consequences of sin include (1) "death" (מות), which is the most frequently prescribed penalty for sin (e.g., Lev 10:1–2); (2) "cutting off" (כרת), which may mean excommunication from the covenant community (e.g., Exod 30:33) or premature death (e.g., Exod 31:14); (3) "bearing sin" (נשא עון), which is a general statement emphasizing that sinners will suffer the punitive consequences of sin (e.g., Lev 20:20); and (4) "becoming guilty" (אשם), which may indicate the recognition of one's guilt.[20]

The first three penalties for sin (death, cutting off, bearing sin) frequently occur in the context of intentional sin, which cannot be forgiven. The last one (becoming guilty) appears in the context of sin that may be atoned for.[21] In the latter case, expiatory sacrifice must be properly offered, otherwise, punitive consequences of sin will continue to lead the sinner to death as stated in Lev 17:11. This verse indicates that the blood of the atoning sacrifice serves to ransom the offender's life, which otherwise is at risk because of sin. In the priestly literature, there is a strong connection between sin and death. Sin, whether it is intentional or inadvertent, leads to death if not addressed properly.

---

judicial sense. For the debate on this issue, see Sklar, *Sin, Impurity, Sacrifice, Atonement*, 12.

20. Boda, *A Severe Mercy*, 60; Kiuchi, *Leviticus*, 68–70. Sklar's rendering is "to suffer guilt's consequences." See also Sklar, *Sin, Impurity, Sacrifice, Atonement*, 24–41.

21. The verb אשם appears 11 times in Leviticus 4, with 5 out of 13 occurrences in the priestly literature: Lev 4:13, 22, 27; 5:2, 3, 4, 5, 17, 19 (2 times) and 23 (MT); Num 5:6, 7. Sklar, *Sin, Impurity, Sacrifice, Atonement*, 24.

Atonement and Forgiveness

As noted above, sinners who have committed unintentional sins may only escape death by means of sacrificial atonement, which is an essential element of the purification and reparation sacrifices. At the end of each expiatory offering, a forgiveness formula is announced to signify the objective of the sacrifice: "so the priest shall make atonement for them, and they will be forgiven" (וכפר עלהם הכהן ונסלח להם:); Lev 4:20; cf. 4:26, 31, 35; 5:10, 13, 18; 6:7 [MT: 5:26]). This concluding statement includes two important verbs: כפר (to make atonement) and נסלח (to be forgiven), with כפר as the prerequisite to נסלח. Having established the role of the offerer in the sacrificial process, I turn to the roles played by the priest (כפר) and by God (נסלח).

The Meaning of כפר in Old Testament Sacrifice

The meaning of כפר (to make atonement) has been understood variously. Traditionally, scholars have appealed to Arabic *kafara* to supply כפר (*kipper*) with a sense of "to cover." Thus, the priest covers the sinner so that the sinner does not have to face the wrath of God.[22] However, this approach, which focuses upon the "original" meaning of the word in order to determine the word's meaning in a later context, has received criticism.[23]

Recently, there has been general consensus among biblical scholars that sees a close connection between כִּפֶּר (to atone) and כֹּפֶר (ransom) when used in the context of sin. Often, כִּפֶּר (*kipper*) is understood in terms of כֹּפֶר (*koper*). While כֹּפֶר (*koper*) means "ransom," then כִּפֶּר (*kipper*) should be interpreted as "to pay ransom."[24] In addition, Milgrom affirms the relatedness of כִּפֶּר (*kipper*) and כֹּפֶר (*koper*): "There exists a strong possibility that all texts that assign to *kipper* [כִּפֶּר] the

---

22. Brown, *Enhanced Brown-Driver-Briggs Hebrew and English Lexicon*, 497.
23. Sklar, *Sin, Impurity, Sacrifice, Atonement*, 44–45.
24. Ibid., 46.

function of averting God's wrath have *koper* [כֹּפֶר] in mind."[25] Thus, to identify the usage of כֹּפֶר (ransom) in the context of sin can shed light on the function of כִּפֶּר (to atone) in the expiatory sacrifice.

Through careful exegesis of passages that contain כֹּפֶר (ransom), those elements central to the sense of this term can be identified. The well-known case of the goring ox (Exod 21:28–32) is one of the כֹּפֶר passages, which indicates clearly that: (1) the wrong of the guilty party has broken the relationship with the injured; (2) the life of the ox owner is forfeited in order to compensate for the loss of the suffering party; (3) however, whether a כֹּפֶר (ransom) is accepted instead of death is up to the injured to decide; (4) if כֹּפֶר (ransom) is granted as the mitigated penalty, then the כֹּפֶר (ransom) functions not only to rescue the life of the guilty, but also to appease the injured; and (5) as a result, the damaged relationship is restored in peace. The exegesis of other related כֹּפֶר passages (Exod 30:11–16; Num 35:30–34; Ps 49:8–9; Prov 6:20–35; 1 Sam 12:1–5; Amos 5:12; Isa 43:3–4; and Job 33:24) also reveals the above fundamental elements of כֹּפֶר (ransom).[26]

In sum, these elements delineate כֹּפֶר (ransom) as a legitimate payment, which is a mitigated penalty accepted by the offended party that delivers the guilty party from the original punishment that the sin warranted, i.e. death. Therefore, כֹּפֶר (ransom) is a price for life (Job 33:24; Exod 30:12). This lesser payment serves to rescue the life of the guilty and to appease the offended party, aiming at restoring peace to the disturbed relationship.

The word כִּפֶּר (to atone) not only means to pay the ransom, but also to purge the impurity. In the priestly literature, כִּפֶּר (to atone) often occurs in conjunction with and relates closely to three states: the impure (טמא), the pure (טהר), and the holy (קדש). This connection suggests that כִּפֶּר (to atone) also plays an important role in the context of purification and consecration.

---

25. Milgrom, *Leviticus 1–16*, 1082.
26. For detailed analysis of each passage, see Sklar, *Sin, Impurity, Sacrifice, Atonement*, 52–59.

The contamination of sin affects the offender and also the sacred space. Therefore, the blood ritual is required, according to Sklar's study, to cleanse/consecrate in order to make the offender pure (טהר) and holy (קדש) again.²⁷ Hence, they have been restored to a state suitable for a relationship with the holy God.²⁸ This function of the כִּפֶּר rite, suggested by Sklar, differs significantly from the influential theory of Milgrom, who insists that the blood-ritual only purifies the sanctuary, but not the offerer, who has been purified at the point of repentence.²⁹ Nevertheless, Gane shares Sklar's view and argues that the privative מִן (from) of מחטאתו (from his sin) in the forgiveness formula (Lev 4:26) indicates that purification offerings can remove evils from their offerers.³⁰

27. The following example relates to the pure (טהר) state: "But if she cannot afford a lamb, then she shall take two turtledoves or two young pigeons, the one for a burnt offering and the other for a sin offering; and the priest shall make atonement (וכפר) for her, and she will be clean (וטהרה)" (Lev 12:8). The following example relates to the holy (קדש) state: "Thus they shall eat those things [refering to the ram of ordination that was offered on Aaron and his sons' behalf] by which atonement (כפר) was made at their ordination and consecration (לקדש אתם; literally: to consecrate them); but a layman shall not eat them, because they are holy" (Exod 29:33). See Sklar, *Sin, Impurity, Sacrifice, Atonement*, 105–36.

28. Based on Exod 24:3–8, Gilders has an alternative view on the blood ritual: "The sprinkling of blood toward or in the abode of Yahweh's presence is a relational-indexing act, indicating a relationship between the head priest and Yahweh, as well as between Yahweh and the community, which the priest represents inside the shrine. His blood manipulation activity indexes the priest as a mediator between the people and Yahweh" (Gilders, *Blood Ritual*, 140–41). Gilders's suggestion is in line with the finding in this paper that the ritual aims at the restoration of relationship between the Lord and the offerer.

29. Milgrom, *Studies in Cultic Theology*, 75–81; Milgrom, *Leviticus 1–16*, 254–58.

30. He argues that the privative מִן (from) of מחטאתו (literally: from his sin) in the forgiveness formula: "The priest shall make atonement (וכפר) for him in regard to his sin (מחטאתו), and he will be forgiven (ונסלח)" indicates that the expiatory offering can purify the offerer (Lev 4:26; cf. 5:10) (Gane, *Leviticus, Numbers*, 104–5). Also, see his detailed analysis in Gane, *Cult Character*, 106–43; 198–202. Boda agrees that priestly rituals facilitate movement from impure to pure or from pure to holy, while sin and impurity cause movement from holy to pure or from pure to impure. He says that "there

This purification process is exhibited symbolically in the expiatory offering. In Lev 4:5–7, the anointed priest sprinkles the blood seven times before the curtain that separates the outer sanctum from the inner sanctum, places some of the blood on the horns of the incense altar, and pours out the rest of the blood at the base of the altar of burnt offering, thus ritually purifying the entire tent of meeting and the outer courtyard, which have been defiled because of sin. The blood ritual is critical and varies according to the status of the offerer (cf. 4:16–18, 25, 30, and 34). The inadvertent sins of the anointed priest are so serious that their negative consequences not only affect the anointed priest himself, but also the whole community that he serves, thus disrupting their relationship with God. These sins also defile ritually the entire sanctuary, right up to the curtain that marks symbolically the entrance to the Holy of Holies, thus threatening the intimate presence of God on earth. The dispersal of the blood provides a ritual way of cleansing both people and sanctuary of the sins and thus making them hospitable again for God.[31]

In summary, in the sacrificial system, כִּפֶּר (to atone) has a strong relationship with כֹּפֶר (ransom) so that כִּפֶּר (to atone) is understood as the effecting of a כֹּפֶר payment on behalf of the guilty. The offended (God) agrees to accept a substitute (a כֹּפֶר), which is the life of the sacrifice. Although the mitigated punishment is still costly to the offender, it is much less so when compared with the deserved penalty, as the consequence of sin is usually death.

---

is a fuzzy line between physical ritual impurity and moral sin" (Boda, *A Severe Mercy*, 58).

The concept of purification is foregrounded vividly on the Day of Atonement when the non-sacrificial goat carries away the impurity of the community from the sanctuary. According to Boda: "The function, then, of the Day of Atonement rituals was to purify the sanctuary and its sancta of impurities and sins (Lev 16:16, 18, 19, 33) and as a result purify the people (Lev 16:30). Defiant sins could not be remedied for the individual by the sacrificial system, but because these sins defile the sanctuary and the community as a whole, a remedy for this impurity was provided once a year on the Day of Atonement" (Boda, *A Severe Mercy*, 74).

31. Balentine, *Leviticus*, 42–43.

Sins pollute the land and major impurities endanger life, therefore, the כָּפֶר rite needs to address purgation as well. Because the sacred space and the offender are purified, they can resume the state of being pure (טהר) and holy (קדש) that is required for God's presence.

In this manner, כָּפֶר (to atone) should mean כֹּפֶר purgation, which mainly addresses the consequence of sin. The ransoming power of blood enables כָּפֶר (to atone) to rescue the offerers from the consequence of sin and the purifying power of blood enables כָּפֶר (to atone) to cleanse their impurity. Finally, the כָּפֶר rite (atonement) results in סלח (forgiveness). Hence, sinners can reconcile with God and restore their relationship.

The Meaning of נסלח in Old Testament Sacrifice

Following the completion of the expiatory sacrifice, ונסלח (then he shall be forgiven) appears together with כָּפֶר (to make atonement) in some variation as a forgiveness formula: "so the priest shall make atonement for them, and they will be forgiven" (וכפר עלהם הכהן ונסלח להם:; Lev 4:20). The Niphal ונסלח in priestly literature is a prompt to search for the subject who grants the forgiveness. It is commonly agreed that forgiveness comes from the Lord, the one who is also the subject of סלח (to forgive) elsewhere in the Old Testament. In the entire Hebrew Bible, only God acts to סלח (forgive), never humans. The use of the passive form here may indicate that, although the priest carries out the כָּפֶר rites, only God can determine their efficacy by forgiving sin.[32] The Lord himself has provided the sacrificial system as a means for sinners to obtain forgiveness.

The Niphal perfect ונסלח (then he shall be forgiven) occurs 13 times in the Old Testament in a context where a sin has been committed and a sacrifice is made.[33] Levine, drawing on Ugaritic and Akkadian cognates, proposes that סלח should mean "to wash, sprinkle with water"; thus, the basic sense would be

---

32. Milgrom, *Leviticus 1–16*, 245.
33. See Lev 4:20, 26, 31, 35; 5:10, 13, 16, 18; 6:7 [MT: 5:26]; 19:22; Num 15:25, 26, 28. Except 6:7 [MT: 5:26] and 19:22, all the sins listed are unintentional.

that of cleansing away with water.[34] His understanding of סלח is quite similar to the human concept of pardon, which includes not only the sense of ceasing from anger, but also the sense of not punishing.[35] However, Milgrom states that the concept of סלח in the Hebrew Bible is far more complex and is different from any anthropopathic notions of forgiveness that humans are capable of giving. Milgrom states that the rendering "to forgive" for סלח is not exactly accurate.[36]

When God grants pardon (סלחתי) in Num 14:20 in response to Moses' petition for forgiveness (סלח־נא) in Num 14:19, the סלח granted cannot connote forgiveness in the human sense since punishment is immediately announced (Num 14:21–24; cf. 14:32–33). When Moses invokes God's attribute in Num 14:18 as a foundation of his petition in v. 19, he clearly does not refer to forgiveness in the human sense: "The Lord is slow to anger and abundant in lovingkindness, forgiving iniquity and transgression; but He will by no means clear *the guilty*" (לא ינקה ונקה; or better, "but he surely will not leave unpunished")".[37] Moses understands that sinners must bear the punitive consequences of sins, though punishments can be substituted by mitigated penalties through the כפר arrangement if the offended (God) agrees.[38] What he pleads is that God be reconciled with his people. This connotation of סלח is further supported in the golden calf narrative when God responds to Moses' request for סלח by renewing the covenant (Exod 34:9–10). Therefore, the offender is longing for and dependent upon God's divine forgiveness (סלח) in order to restore the broken relationship. Reconciliation is the ultimate goal of the expiatory sacrifice.

The consonance between סלח (to forgive) and נשא עון (to bear sin) finds support when these two terms are used

---

34. Levine, *Leviticus*, 24.
35. As in the *Cambridge Advanced Learner's Dictionary*.
36. Milgrom, *Leviticus 1–16*, 245.
37. Brown, *Enhanced Brown-Driver-Briggs Hebrew and English Lexicon*, 667; Koehler et al., *The Hebrew and Aramaic Lexicon of the Old Testament*, 720.
38. The punishment of the repentant sinner might be due either to divine retribution, or to natural consequences. See note 20.

interchangeably in some instances. In Exod 32:32, when Moses asks the Lord to forgive the sin of the people (חטאתם תשא) after the golden calf incident, the phrase נשא חטא (to bear sin) is used with the meaning "to forgive sin."[39] In Exod 34:7, when God is described as the one "who forgives iniquity, transgression, and sin" (נשא עון ופשע וחטאה) in his self-revelation, the phrase נשא עון פשע חטא (to bear iniquity, transgression, and sin) employed has the connotation of forgiveness of sin. Thus, by examining the meaning of נשא עון (to bear sin), we can have a better understanding of סלח (to forgive).

The phrase נשא עון occurs in three distinct contexts: (1) the sinner is the subject of the verb, thus נשא עון means "to bear punishment"; (2) the offended is the subject of the verb, thus the offended agrees to bear the sin consequence, hence, נשא עון may be translated as "to forgive sin"; (3) a third party is the subject of the verb, thus נשא עון can render as "to bear away punishment."

In this study, it is the second usage of נשא עון, where the offended is the subject, that can shed light on the nature of divine forgiveness (סלח). In the context of sacrifice, the offended is the Lord, who bears our sin consequences (נשא עון) when he grants סלח after the כפר rite.[40] Although we do not know exactly how God bears our punishment, the consonance between סלח and נשא עון demonstrates that God is deeply affected by bearing the cost of forgiveness.

There is one thing common to all verses with נשא עון (to bear sin) used in the second sense, some form of punishment will follow the divine forgiveness announced in the immediate context. The coexistence of punishment and forgiveness is fully demonstrated in Numbers 14. In Num 14:20, the Lord said to Moses, "I have pardoned (סלחתי) according to your word," which does not mean Israel will escape all the punishment they

---

39. נשא may be conjoined with various terms for sin: פשע, חטא, עון. These terms used in the contexts of sin that I am referring to do not have much difference in meaning, and thus for the sake of simplicity, they are treated as the same in my discussion.

40. Sklar, *Sin, Impurity, Sacrifice, Atonement*, 88–90.

deserve. As in Num 14:21–23, the Lord proceeds to declare that those rebellious adults will die in the wilderness.[41] Thus סלח does not necessarily refer to the complete remission of punishment, but allows for a lesser penalty. In the case of Numbers 14, the original penalty is the wiping out of the entire nation immediately as mentioned in 14:11–12, while the mitigated penalty only affects the adults during their forty years wandering in the wilderness (14:29).

In light of this, it is evident that whenever sinners request that the offended נשא עון (forgive sin), they are pleading for a remission of the original penalty that the sin deserves. This substitution of a mitigated penalty in lieu of the deserved one is congruent with the כִּפֶּר principle mentioned above.

In summary, the כִּפֶּר rite results in divine forgiveness (סלח). The Niphal סלח suggests that only God can bring about the efficacy of the ritual by granting forgiveness. The connotation of סלח is different from any anthropopathic notions of pardon. It aims at reconciliation. The sinner performs an expiatory sacrifice in order to restore the disturbed relationship with God.

In the context of the sacrificial system, the second usage of נשא עון (to forgive sin) indicates that the Lord, as the offended when people sin, bears away the punitive consequence that the sin deserves by granting divine forgiveness (סלח) to the offender through the כִּפֶּר arrangement, with the result that the sinner does not suffer the original penalty, which would probably lead to death. As a result, the כִּפֶּר rite functions to reconcile the two parties, thus restoring peace to the relationship.

Implications

The Seriousness of the Consequences of Sin

It is regrettable that we moderns distance ourselves from, or even have disdain for, the priestly tradition. Our estimate and awareness of sin is so low that we are easily enslaved. The priestly understanding of sin is more than an abstraction; it is real and multifaceted. Sin operates at every level of society and

---

41. Ibid., 84–85; Sakenfeld, "Problem of Divine Forgiveness."

no person is exempt from its reach. Sin is serious and has consequences. At the personal and communal level, sin disrupts relationships within community. We now live in alienation from the world around us, without harmony.[42] Sin is like a pollutant discharged into the atmosphere and its destructive force can destroy societies and institutions.

The sins of the faith community can be even more serious, for they corrupt and defile sacred space—the body of Christ—thus threatening enjoyment of the presence of God and the solidarity of the community as a whole. As a result, the church becomes a lamp under a basket, which cannot shine before men (Matt 5:15), and hence, its prophetic voice continues to recede from the world. Today, the priestly literature continually warns us, who are God's covenant people, that sin not only leads to death and disrupts relationship with God, but also diminishes our capacity to be the blessing we were created to be.[43]

The Hope of Divine Forgiveness
The priestly tradition does not leave us in despair over sin, but gives us hope in God. The forgiveness formula: "so the priest shall make atonement for them, and they will be forgiven" (Lev 4:20) is repeated consistently in order to emphasize that the objective of the expiatory offering is divine forgiveness (סלח). God takes the initiative to be reconciled with his people. The Old Testament sacrifice invites sinners to repent and return to the loving God who is the *only* source of life and blessing. Genuine forgiveness and reconciliation can be found in God *alone*.

The passive form of סלח (to forgive) reminds the faith community that the agent of forgiveness is always God. Only God can grant forgiveness.[44] This concept that forgiveness belongs to the Lord is fully embraced in the New Testament. When Jesus said to the paralytic, "Son, your sins are forgiven" (Mark 2:5), the teachers of the law immediately accused him as a blasphemer and posed the question: "Who can forgive sins *but God alone?*"

---

42. Grenz, *Theology*, 268–69.
43. Balentine, *Leviticus*, 52–53.
44. Ibid., 54.

(Mark 2:7, italics mine). They were correct in that, according to their scriptural tradition, forgiveness is granted by God alone.[45]

This forgiveness demands our own reconciliation with those who have offended us. God retains the right to forgiveness for two main reasons. First, the act of forgiving is sometimes difficult to be practiced by finite humans alone. Without forgiveness, reconciliation is impossible. Second, the forgiveness granted by God is different from any human notion of forgiveness. For human beings, forgiveness might not always lead to reconciliation, as contended by Childs: "Forgiveness is not the equivalent of reconciliation, however, it is the means to which barriers to reconciliation (which may or may not follow) are removed."[46] Nevertheless, the divine forgiveness dispensed by God aims at restoring broken relationships. Divine forgiveness allows us to move beyond forgiveness into genuine reconciliation, which is the ultimate goal of expiatory sacrifice. Reconciliation is possible as divine forgiveness flows together with grace, where mercy can triumph over justice. The forgiving mercy of God can provide healing power to the parties involved, though the actual healing process may be different from case to case.[47] That is why Leviticus reiterates the call to turn to God, the source of divine forgiveness, in rectifying the consequences of sin and restoring the broken relationship.

It is clear that God is not content with a mere vertical view of forgiveness. Instead, as with his other gifts, he wants his new creation to share his forgiveness with those around us: "forgiving each other . . . just as the Lord forgave you, so also should you" (Col 3:13; cf. Eph 4:32). How can we forgive if forgiveness belongs to the Lord? The answer is "just as the Lord forgave you, so also should you." When we forgive according to the Scriptures, we are extending God's forgiveness, received by us, to other people by reconciling with them (cf. 1 Cor 4:6). This is exhibited in 1 John 4:7–11: "Beloved, let us love one another,

---

45. See Gane, *Leviticus, Numbers*, 64–65.
46. Childs, "Forgiveness," 438, cited in DeVries, "From Vertical to Horizontal," 17.
47. See DeVries, "From Vertical to Horizontal," 17–18.

for love is from God . . . The one who does not love does not know God, for God is love . . . Beloved, *if God so loved us, we also ought to love one another*" (italics mine). In the same manner, if we have experienced God's forgiving gift, we should share God's grace with others. The faith community should be the channel of God's love, grace, and forgiveness.

To extend God's forgiveness is not a suggestion but a demand. For the faith community, horizontal forgiveness does not only originate from the vertical dimension of forgiveness, but is also a prerequisite for the vertical. This concept was clearly exhibited in the reparation offering, which required sinners to rectify their relationship with others before they could secure forgiveness from the Lord (Lev 6:5–6 [MT: 5:24–25]). The same principle is also found in Matt 5:23–24: "Therefore if you are presenting your offering at the altar, and there remember that your brother has something against you, leave your offering there before the altar and go; first be reconciled to your brother, and then come and present your offering." Jesus further explains the significance of this theme: "And forgive us our debts, *as we also have forgiven our debtors* . . . But if you do not forgive others, then your Father will not forgive your transgressions" (Matt 6:12–15, italics mine). The parable of the unmerciful servant (Matt 18:23–35) provides a warning that if we do not forgive others, we will face God's judgment: "My heavenly Father will also do the same to you, if each of you does not forgive his brother from your heart" (Matt 18:35).

From the above discussion, we find that forgiveness and community depend on each other. The church came into existence through the divine forgiveness flowing out from the cross. However, within the church, divine forgiveness continues to be dispensed when we embrace each other.[48] The rejection of our brothers and sisters removes the foundation of God's forgiveness. The Scriptures proclaim that the Lord is a forgiving God (Exod 34:7; Num 14:18). He wants his people to imitate him by having a forgiving attitude. He loves to see the faith community

---

48. See Clayton, "Forgiveness," 11–12.

relating with each other in peace and harmony just like the Triune God.[49]

Since forgiveness is God's gift extended through his people, shall we "continue in sin so that grace may increase?" (Rom 6:1). Just as Paul responded to this question, "May it never be!" (Rom 6:2), Leviticus removes the illusion of cheap forgiveness. The כִּפֶּר rite is a gift provided by God only to the repenting offender who suffers from the consequence of sin and longs for reconciliation with God and his created world. The complicated procedure of the expiatory offering was a continual reminder that forgiveness is not to be taken for granted. During the process, all parties were addressed: (1) the offender (the offerer) needed to confess and pay the penalty, (2) the offended (God) accepted the כִּפֶּר arrangement and agreed to forgive, (3) other injured parties were compensated in full according to the legislation, and (4) the mediator (the priest) represented the community in order to carry out the reconciliation procedure; thus, sin would not endanger the community's survival.

The consonance between סלח (to forgive) and נשא עון (to bear sin) suggests that God is deeply affected by bearing the cost of forgiveness. Divine forgiveness is a deliberate choice and is costly, which was fully exhibited when God absorbed the prerequisite cost in the sacrifice of his Son.[50] The Old Testament sacrifice highlights mercy and justice as crucial components of God's love. Mercy can only be an effective form of discipline if the one being disciplined understands the demand of justice and the cost of the gift of mercy.

Do This in Remembrance of Him[51]

Does the revelation at Sinai still have relevance to the church today? It is true that Old Testament sacrifice, the heart of ancient Israelite worship, could always be reduced to routine ceremony,

---

49. See Grenz, *Theology*, 110–27, for comments regarding the relational God.
50. Gane, *Leviticus, Numbers*, 110.
51. The idea of this section is primarily drawn from Grenz, *Theology*, 697–704.

just as is possible with a variety of significant symbolic acts in Christian worship today. The theological significance of the expiatory offering is so important that Jesus commands his followers to repeatedly reaffirm it. Through participation in the Lord's Supper, the expiatory gift continues to speak to the faith community today.

The Lord's Supper was instituted by Jesus as a perpetual celebration at his last meal with the disciples. When Christians observe the Lord's Supper together, we reenact the Last Supper and fulfill our Lord's command: "do this in remembrance of me" (1 Cor 11:24; cf. 11:25). This memorial aspect draws attention to what God has done for us through his Son's sacrificial death. Through our eating and drinking, we proclaim, in a symbolic manner, that Jesus sacrificed his life for us (1 Cor 11:24–25). This past orientation brings us back to the essence of the expiatory sacrifice that provides the meaning for Jesus' death—he becomes the atonement for human sin and his blood seals a new covenant. The forgiveness formula reminds us that atonement leads to divine forgiveness, which aims at restoration of broken relationships (renewal of covenant). Christ's atoning sacrifice enables God's divine forgiveness to flow in grace to those who long for reconciliation with the loving God and his world.

The sacrificial death of Jesus not only effects a new relationship between us and God but also destroys the barriers dividing human beings (Eph 2:11–22). The vertical and horizontal dimensions of forgiveness in Old Testament sacrifice are fully embraced in Christ's atonement. The church is the eschatological covenant community, called to reflect the nature of the Triune God himself. Whenever we observe the Lord's Supper, the Holy Spirit rekindles our devotion for Christ and strengthens us to "proclaim the Lord's death until he comes" (1 Cor 11:26). When we celebrate God's forgiving grace, we are reminded to extend his grace to other people. The expiatory gift speaks whenever we recount Jesus' death on the cross. It continues to speak when the faith community participates in Christ's reconciling work.

Bibliography

Anderson, Gary A. "Sacrifice and Sacrificial Offerings (OT)." In *ABD* 5:870–86. Edited by David Noel Freedman. 6 vols. New York: Doubleday, 1992.

Balentine, Samuel E. *Leviticus. Interpretation: A Bible Commentary for Teaching and Preaching*. Louisville: John Knox, 2002.

Boda, Mark J. *A Severe Mercy: Sin and Its Remedy in the Old Testament*. Siphrut 1. Winona Lake: Eisenbrauns, 2009.

Brown, Francis, et al. *Enhanced Brown-Driver-Briggs Hebrew and English Lexicon*. Electronic edition. Oak Harbor, WA: Logos Research Systems, 2000.

Budd, Philip J. *Leviticus*. NCBC. Grand Rapids: Eerdmans, 1996.

Cambridge Advanced Learner's Dictionary. 3rd ed. Cambridge: Cambridge University Press, 2008. Accessed March 11, 2009. Online: http://dictionary.cambridge.org/.

Childs, B. H. "Forgiveness." In *Dictionary of Pastoral Care and Counseling*, edited by Rodney J. Hunter, 438–40. Nashville: Abingdon, 1990.

Clayton, Timothy. "Forgiveness: An Ecclesiological Act." Unpublished Essay, McMaster Divinity College, Hamilton, ON, 2009.

DeVries, Joan. "From Vertical to Horizontal Forgiveness: Expanding the Contours." Unpublished Essay, McMaster Divinity College, Hamilton, ON, 2009.

Douglas, Mary. *Leviticus as Literature*. Oxford: Oxford University Press, 1999.

Gane, Roy. *Cult Character: Purification Offerings, Day of Atonement, and Theodicy*. Winona Lake: Eisenbrauns, 2005.

———. *Leviticus, Numbers*. NIVAC. Grand Rapids: Zondervan, 2004.

Gilders, William K. *Blood Ritual in the Hebrew Bible: Meaning and Power*. Baltimore: Johns Hopkins University Press, 2004.

Grenz, Stanley J. *Theology for the Community of God*. Nashville: Broadman & Holman, 1994.

Kiuchi, Nobuyoshi. *Leviticus*. Apollos Old Testament Commentary 3. Downers Grove, IL: InterVarsity, 2007.

Koehler, Ludwig, et al. *The Hebrew and Aramaic Lexicon of the Old Testament*. 4 vols. Leiden: Brill, 1999.

Levine, Baruch A. *Leviticus*. JPS Torah Commentary. Philadelphia: Jewish Publication Society, 1989.

Milgrom, Jacob. *Cult and Conscience: The Asham and the Priestly Doctrine of Repentance*. Studies in Judaism in Late Antiquity. Leiden: Brill, 1976.

———. *Leviticus 1–16: A New Translation with Introduction and Commentary*. AB. New York: Doubleday, 1991.

———. *Studies in Cultic Theology and Terminology*. Studies in Judaism in Late Antiquity. Leiden: Brill, 1983.

Sakenfeld, Katharine D. "The Problem of Divine Forgiveness in Numbers 14." *CBQ* 37 (1975) 317–30.

Sklar, Jay. *Sin, Impurity, Sacrifice, Atonement: The Priestly Conceptions*. Hebrew Bible Monographs 2. Sheffield: Sheffield Phoenix, 2005.

A SINGLE HORIZON HERMENEUTICS: A PROPOSAL FOR
INTERPRETIVE IDENTIFICATION

Stanley E. Porter
McMaster Divinity College

Introduction

The concept of the two horizons of interpretation—the original horizon of the author or text and the contemporary horizon of the interpreter—has become a standard paradigm in Western hermeneutical thought. This notion of two horizons is clearly the product of Enlightenment thought and the development of modern critical thinking. First adumbrated by Friedrich Schleiermacher,[1] the concept of the two horizons was perhaps most forcefully articulated by Hans-Georg Gadamer in his *Truth and Method* (a book with questionable claims about both),[2] and then widely accepted and developed by numerous others. Even within evangelical hermeneutical thought (my primary though not exclusive audience for this paper), the notion of two horizons has become a standard interpretive paradigm. For example, Anthony Thiselton's arguably best known hermeneutical work is entitled *The Two Horizons*, after the concept articulated by Gadamer,[3] and Grant Osborne plays with the fixed notion by creating reciprocity in his book on general hermeneutics, *The*

---

1. See Porter and Robinson, *Hermeneutics*, ch. 1.
2. First published in 1960 in German, and then in English translation in 1975, and again in 2002. For a recent treatment of Gadamer, see Porter and Robinson, *Hermeneutics*, ch. 9.
3. Thiselton bases his title upon Gadamer, who is one of the four major figures that he discusses in the volume, along with Heidegger, Bultmann, and Wittgenstein.

Hermeneutical Spiral.[4] At first blush, the notion of two horizons seems to be a reasonable one, even an ineluctable one; modern interpreters recognize and appreciate the hermeneutical distance between their own horizon of understanding and the horizon of the (at least in biblical studies) ancient author and text. The former is governed by the presuppositions and assumptions of the interpreter's modern world and context, while the latter may include ancient Israel of the patriarchal, pre-exilic, or post-exilic period; or the Palestinian, Mediterranean, or even European worlds of the New Testament.[5] It is fair to say that there have been many interesting and useful insights that have emerged from such a perspective. These include, not least, the hermeneutical appreciation of distance, otherness, and difference, and the need to find means of bridging the chronological, cultural, and perspectival breach between the two horizons and their concomitant worlds.[6] Such has been the approach of modern Western biblical criticism since the rise of the historical-critical method,[7] even by further developments into criticisms that wish to disregard the potential minimalism of modern interpretive approaches (such as canonical or literary criticism).[8] However, there have also been severe and perhaps even harmful limitations

---

4. Osborne's emphasis is more upon the interactive process by which horizons supposedly interact, thus resulting in a spiral. He is followed by, among others, Klein et al., *Introduction*.

5. There have, of course, been other hermeneutical paradigms, including the single horizon hermeneutics of Rudolf Bultmann, who essentially dismisses the horizon of the author/text and reads in terms of only his own (highly limited and strictly materialist) horizon, seen especially in his program of demythologization. See Bultmann, "New Testament and Mythology." It is arguable that many, if not most, forms of historical/higher criticism utilize a single horizon hermeneutics of the modern interpreter, even if not as extremely as does Bultmann.

6. These are preoccupations of recent modernist and post-modernist thought. See Porter and Robinson, *Hermeneutics*, ch. 7 (structuralism) and ch. 8 (Derrida and deconstruction).

7. For histories of the historical-critical method in Old Testament see Reventlow, *History of Biblical Interpretation*, and in New Testament, Baird, *History of New Testament Research*.

8. See Porter and Robinson, *Hermeneutics*, ch. 11 (literary hermeneutics).

that have resulted from such a hermeneutical approach. Along with distance, otherness, and difference, there has come interpretive and hermeneutical alienation,[9] loss of biblical confidence,[10] and theological anxiety.[11]

Despite such supposed interpretive advances as those promoted by the two horizons, there are those elsewhere in the contemporary world for whom such modern and even post-modern angst are not the realities of their hermeneutical and hence interpretive agenda. In a recent lecture at McMaster Divinity College,[12] Philip Jenkins made the important point (recounted here in my own words and interpretation) that miracles and other extra-normal phenomena are almost a commonplace among Christians in the majority world, such as sub-Saharan Africa. For them, the Bible is not an alien or ancient document but, they believe, one written literally for them, in that the context of the Bible is their shared and relevant context.[13] In other words, what I think that Jenkins is indicating—and those in such hermeneutical contexts are realizing, even if inadvertently and without the ability necessarily to express it in these words—is that, in such interpretive contexts, the Bible and the modern interpreter share a single horizon. There is a single horizon hermeneutics in play. There are not two horizons that formalize and even perpetuate the interpretive divide between author/text and interpreter. Instead, there is a single horizon of author/text/interpreter, in which the horizon of creation and reception, promulgation and expectation, is common and shared. One might say that more is shared than even a creative and expectative horizon. It may be

---

9. I.e., the world of the original text is foreign and distant from the contemporary interpretive context.

10. I.e., modern thought is by definition viewed as fuller, superior and deeper, requiring adjustment of expectations regarding the necessarily more primitive and simpler (if not simplistic) earlier biblical text and its people.

11. This occurs when one realizes the difficulty of making an ancient and, dare one say, now dead text speak to a modern and living context.

12. Philip Jenkins was the guest of McMaster Divinity College to deliver three plenary lectures at a conference, "Globalization of Christian Faith and Ministry," on 11 June 2011.

13. Jenkins makes a similar point in Jenkins, *New Faces*, esp. 4–7.

that there is, at least perceived to be, a similar cultural, religious, economic, educational, and political horizon (not horizons) between the two. This horizon would possibly include ethnic identification in the context of foreign intrusion, religious exclusivity within a broader panoply of other incompatible fervent religious belief, economic struggle and divide between the many who have not and the few who have, educational deprivation for many and privilege for few, and political oppression and struggle. I do not think that—assuming one can use such widespread generalities—it is unfair to say that the majority world of today has far more in common in almost all regards with the ancient world of the Bible, whether of the Old or New Testaments, than the modern Western world. The majority world, with its struggle for existence against oppressive antagonists and its pre-modern orientation to life, is very much more similar to the ancient world than is the post-Christian and post-religious, and even post-post-modern (and still very modern), West.[14]

The Proposal of a Single Horizon Hermeneutics against Other Hermeneutical Approaches

This interpretive situation, if I am even close to being right (and I believe that I am, at least to the point of promoting the topic for discussion), suggests that we may need to examine in more detail a single horizon hermeneutics. Such a hermeneutics values, validates, and even embraces the interpretive commonalities of the biblical world and the modern world, rather than continuing to advocate for a divided and alienated world of two horizons—always at a distance, and struggling for the first to be heard and appreciated against the backdrop of the skepticism of the second. A single horizon hermeneutics would endorse the notion that the

---

14. I acknowledge that such terms as modernism, post-modernism, and post-Christian are potentially problematic, but are here clear enough. I also sense that what many of us recognized from the start—the difficulty of the term post-modern (what comes after it?)—is now coming to bear upon our situation—we have moved beyond post-modernism, or, perhaps better, come to recognize that what we used to call post-modernism is just another sub-category of what we should probably still call modernism.

operative essentials of the biblical world should be taken seriously. These include the fact of God's existence,[15] his actual and historical revelation in Jesus Christ through incarnation,[16] the reality of God's work in the world by diverse means (not just the notional possibility but the reality of what are usually called miracles—and not as some kind of hypothetical possibility of violation of natural law, but the reality that God's world includes laws of his own making),[17] the reality of resurrection of which Jesus Christ's was the first of many to come,[18] and similar truths.

A single horizon hermeneutics would recognize that many of the developments in the post-biblical world have not genuinely enhanced understanding and application, or even general appreciation, of the biblical text. These developments have instead served in various ways to alienate the text from its primary readers, those who wish to call themselves Christians and follow the teachings of Jesus Christ as God's perfect human expression of himself. A single horizon hermeneutics is of course not the panacea of all interpretive difficulties, because the biblical text, even if it is seen to share the same horizon as that of the biblical reader and even scholar, still requires interpretation, then as it does now. However, this interpretation is performed in an admittedly

---

15. I will refrain from comment about the so-called New Atheism, which is not new and not even thoroughgoing atheism, in that it worships its own inerrant gods (such as human reason, materialism, and the like). If instead labeled the New Paganism, many might more readily perceive it for what it is. See Overman, *Case for the Existence of God*; and Plantinga and Wolterstorff, *Faith and Rationality*.

16. See Taylor, *Names of Jesus*, a now widely neglected but still valuable study.

17. See Brown, *Miracles and the Critical Mind*; and for a recent treatment in relation to the biblical audience, Keener, *Miracles*.

18. See Licona, *Resurrection of Jesus*. There has been much unnecessary squawking regarding some of his minor conclusions, but I think the work is overall very sound in method and conclusions. Although I certainly agree with Wright's conclusions in *Resurrection* regarding the reality of Jesus Christ's resurrection, one does not need the full 800 pages he takes to prove it, especially as many of the pages are for the most part extraneous to the case he makes. See the review of Bedard, Review of Wright, *Resurrection*.

complex way in the context of a shared horizon of interpretive expectations and assumptions, rather than from a distinctly different and even alienated horizon diachronically and synchronically removed.

Some may believe, however, that some previously articulated hermeneutical models have already addressed many, if not most, of the issues briefly introduced in this short excursion into hermeneutical thought. Two models that come to mind, and often linked together, are canonical approaches or canonical readings, and so-called theological interpretation.[19] There are many potentially good things to say about these interpretive strategies and their desire to address the theological distance of modern interpretation. However, I do not believe that they address the heart of the issue outlined in this article.

Canonical readings, especially those influenced by the work of Brevard Childs, and perhaps the most important New Testament practitioner of his method, Robert Wall,[20] address the issue of the integrity and unity of the canonical biblical text as the maximal hermeneutical context. They recognize it as a product of the church, and interpret it in light of the church's claim upon it. Canonical readers are often sensitive to the shape and development of the canon, and how these factors influence the reading of the Bible. However, canonical readings, for all of their interpretive strength, are still subject to the historical distance and even tension found in modern critical readings—hence they resort to the canon as hermeneutical context. Childs was an accomplished historical critic who never wished to create a disjunction between his approach to the Bible and historical criticism. Similarly, Wall wishes to appropriate the results of historical criticism, even while bracketing out historical conclusions in his

---

19. There are many similarities between these two approaches, although their noteworthy differences should emerge in the discussion that follows.

20. See, for example, Childs, *Introduction to the Old Testament*; Childs, *New Testament as Canon*; Wall and Lemcio, *New Testament as Canon*. For a recent Old Testament treatment, see Seitz, *Character of Christian Scripture*. There are many other studies as well, especially in Old Testament studies. Wall himself has been the major figure in New Testament studies.

effort to preserve and interpret the text.[21] The major problem is that his bracketing of historical questions concedes that his position as modern interpreter is alien to the historical context of the Bible, and in fact elevates it as superior to the understanding of the ancients, including the first Christians. The interpretation of the Pastoral Epistles presents a well-known example. Rather than accepting them as Pauline letters, as they by all accounts were by the earliest Christians (a point acknowledged even by those who believe them to be pseudepigraphal), canonical criticism has two alternatives. It must either pretend this is not true by imposing a foreign sense of authorship as divorced from historical reality, or even adopt a historical-critical conclusion—that of pseudonymy—and utilize this stance as a means of reading the letters as early interpretations (though canonized) of the genuine Paul.[22] Neither satisfies the requirements of a single horizon hermeneutics, but each falls back on modern horizons of interpretation as a means of dictating to the horizon of the original text and author.

Theological interpretation—whether it is considered a hermeneutical stance or instead a variety of hermeneutical positions that commonly lay hold of pre-modern exegetical and theological conclusions—has been widely heralded as a modern (or perhaps even post-modern) solution to the conundrum of the two horizons, including the possible sterility of historical-critical interpretation.[23] Theological interpretation, though varied in

---

21. This is clear in the exchange that I had with him. See Porter, "Pauline Authorship: Implications"; Wall, "Pauline Authorship"; Porter, "Pauline Authorship: Response."

22. See my latest analysis of this type of approach in Porter, "Implications."

23. Some key works in this area, among many, are Vanhoozer, *Dictionary*; Watson, *Text, Church, and World*; Watson, *Text and Truth*; Fowl, *Engaging Scripture*; Treier, *Introducing Theological Interpretation*; Billings, *Word of God*; Green, *Seized by Truth*; and Green, *Practicing Theological Interpretation*. There has been much theorizing about theological interpretation and, to date, the interpretive results are relatively slender and unconvincing, including the examples in the Two Horizons Commentary Series (the title is descriptive of the purpose). See Porter, "What Difference Does Hermeneutics Make?" Furthermore, it would probably shock some of those included in Fowl, *Theological Interpretation* (edited volume) to be found in such a collection, and the

approach, has as several of its common strands the invocation of pre-modern interpretive conclusions as in some sense determinative for modern interpretation, giving priority to the theological conclusions of the early church especially as found in the great creeds such as that of Nicea, and endorsing the theological interpretation of the church as preserving and transmitting theological truth.[24]

No doubt there is much to welcome in such a position that affirms Christian Trinitarian belief, welcomes the church as an active participant in theological understanding, and recognizes that serious theological thinking about the Bible did not emerge for the first time with the Enlightenment. However, theological interpretation itself embraces a number of problematic assumptions in its efforts to bridge the interpretive chasm of the ancients and moderns. One of the major problems is why in its interpretive regress theological interpretation comes to land firmly in the fourth century or so, or at least on the major creeds. This is not in any way to diminish the importance of the creeds and the role they have played in Christian history and thought. The inherent sentiment seems to be, however, that whereas the biblical account may be theologically diverse and open to divergent interpretation, these creeds are fixed in their meaning. Further, whereas the biblical text is the inspired text of interpretation, the creeds and statements by Fathers of the early church seem to displace them as themselves revealed pronouncements. Nevertheless, these statements themselves are not final interpretations of

---

range of examples in Vanhoozer, *Dictionary*, is surprisingly broad. See also Adam et al., *Reading Scripture*, for further examples. In Bockmuehl, *Seeing the Word*, the author purports to be in this line of interpretation but his reader-response and reception-theory orientation, rather than solving the problem of the two horizons, places interpretation firmly within the modernist agenda, with its concomitant results. A brief (and in this climate, thereby good) summary is found in Fowl, *Theological Interpretation* (Cascade). The roots of this movement are seen in the theological hermeneutics of Thiselton (see Thiselton, *Two Horizons*; Thiselton, *New Horizons*) and Vanhoozer (see Vanhoozer, *Is There a Meaning?*; Vanhoozer, *Drama of Doctrine*). Cf. Porter and Robinson, *Hermeneutics*, ch. 10.

24. For an assessment, see Porter, "What Difference Does Hermeneutics Make?"

issues, but are attempts in an ongoing process of encapsulating and refining the admittedly rich and abundant teaching of the Bible in precise statements suited to their own interpretive contexts. In other words, the creeds and similar formulations, for all of their worth, are at worst time-bound interpretations reflecting the issues around which the councils were called or the statements formulated, and at best excellent, though brief (and perhaps in some cases strangely, if not mis-formulated), statements in the developing thought and application of the Bible to contemporary contexts. That is, the creeds themselves reflect in many ways the same kind of exercise as modern theological interpreters are engaged in. The question is legitimately raised as to why theological interpreters do not revert to the Bible itself, rather than simply focusing upon the fourth century or other early pre-modern interpreters as forming their horizon of interpretation. Furthermore, there is no necessary virtue in allowing the church to have determinative interpretive powers. The Christian church itself is a tremendously important institution, if by that we mean the church instigated by Jesus Christ as his representative means of work in the world. However, the church as usually understood is highly diverse in belief and practice, and not inherently better able to adjudicate interpretation than modern critical thought. One only needs to examine differences between the Eastern and Western churches, disputes over such important institutions as baptism and communion, contentions over church order and office, and even the understandings of major doctrines, such as the Trinity. This list does not even address the significance of the institutionalization of the church in the fourth century and how that politico-theological act radically altered the relation of the church to society—an effect that has never been remedied in the West.[25] Finally, early interpreters such as Augustine, Jerome, and Aquinas, as well as others, for all of their brilliance, were themselves not of one mind, and often had a number of highly contentious theological ideas,

---

25. Leithart, *Defending Constantine*. Constantine was no doubt sincere in his faith, but despite good intentions, the result was highly questionable.

alongside more settled ones.[26] Such ideas are often highly informative, but a far cry from being determinative for theological understanding. Whatever is gained by a return to early Christian interpretation is lost by the realization that there are fewer answers in these hallowed mists of time than there are further questions and paradoxes.

Neither of these proposed solutions seems to be able to rise to the necessary standard of interpretation sought by those who wish to be able to appreciate the theological importance and significance of the Bible. This compels us to explore further the single horizon hermeneutics.

The Ramifications of a Single Horizon Hermeneutics

There are, of course, many questions to be raised by the proposal of a single horizon hermeneutics, especially in this modern, postmodern, or post-post-modern age. We live in an age when foundationalism (whether grounded in propositionalism, idealism, empiricism, or naturalism) has in many ways given way to non-foundationalism (or at least, in some who wish to maintain some of the trappings and security of the old without completely giving over to the new, anti-foundationalism), only now to have a resurgence of a chastened and more circumscribed foundationalism.[27] Despite any protests to the contrary, I believe that attempts to eliminate or transcend hermeneutical horizontal distance are attempts to establish a form of interpretive foundation. The goal is to find a firm basis for defining common interpretive ground, so that there is a means by which one can say that what the ancient text says constitutes a basis of belief that can be transferred or mediated into the modern world. Even more than that, it can provide a platform for contemporaneous faith and practice. In such hermeneutical contexts, more is demanded of

---

26. As Lewis, *Discarded Image*, 49–60, points out in the case of Chalcidius.

27. See Bonnycastle, *In Search of Authority*; Cunningham, *Reading after Theory*; Donoghue, *Practice of Reading*; Sollors, *Thematic Criticism*; and Livingston, *Literary Knowledge*.

interpretation than that we simply appeal to language games, but that such language be grounded in something more, such as the larger functional revelatory context. Contextless speech-acts are inadequate to describe the full range of functionality of language, which is necessary to grasp its meaning-significance.[28] And surely we are past the kinds of simplistic, unvalidatable, and hence invalid assertions of logical positivism or anti-absolutism.

This does not mean that there are not other problems to confront with a single horizon hermeneutics. We must remember that our interpretive stance of today indeed is—and no doubt at least in part because of Enlightenment thought and historical criticism—the product of previous thought. We are at the end of a stream of interpretive history, or the history of reception and response to the formative and foundational texts of our traditions. It is virtually impossible for one to even imagine, to say nothing of implement, a return to pre-Enlightenment thought, to forget the accumulated history of the pre-modern period and modernity and its accomplishments, especially when in order to do so we must utilize and appropriate the very tools that have only come to fruition by means of such modernistic thought and processes. We cannot be expected to forget, or to ignore, previous critical interpretation, and we certainly cannot pretend that all of what has transpired in what we might call the modern world simply never existed. That is an impossibility. Besides this not constituting a hermeneutical stance or resulting in interpretation, this is not what a single horizon hermeneutics demands. A single horizon hermeneutics does not demand that we undo the past or overlook the present, but that we subsume our understanding so as to adopt the same horizon as the text/author that we wish to interpret.

---

28. Attempts have been made along these lines in Thiselton, *Two Horizons*; Thiselton, *New Horizons*; Vanhoozer, *Is There a Meaning?*; Vanhoozer, *Drama of Doctrine*; among other works. See Porter and Robinson, *Hermeneutics*, ch. 10. Cf. Klemke, *Contemporary Analytic and Linguistic Philosophies*.

Single Horizon Hermeneutics and Interpretation

The final issue to address is what exactly a single horizon hermeneutics might look like in practice, and especially in relation to interpretation of the biblical text. As noted above, adopting a single horizon hermeneutics does not mean that one obviates the history of interpretation, denies how texts have been received over time (*Wirkungsgeschichte*), pretends to be an ancient interpreter though living in the present, and flagrantly disregards modern interpretive methods and techniques as if they were never developed and never utilized. To the contrary, all of these elements are still pertinent to—though not definitive of—a single horizon hermeneutics, and can in fact be utilized by a single horizon interpreter to aid in the task of interpretation. The condition of the single horizon hermeneutics is that one does not degrade the status or position of the single horizon of the author/text or exalt the stance and insight of the modern interpreter. Instead, the horizon of the original text is given interpretive precedence as establishing the singular horizon of interpretation, and thereby delimiting the legitimate boundaries of interpretation, defining the questions to be posed to the text, circumscribing the limits of methods to be invoked in interpretation, and establishing the parameters of legitimate interpretation. There is no fusion of horizons that attempts to discover, much less create, an unattainable common ground of interpretation, because such a common ground can never do justice to the perspective of either the author/text or the interpreter. There is also no fusion of horizons that of necessity subordinates the ancient, as inherently limited and parochial, to the more expansive understanding of the present. Single horizon hermeneutics recognizes that other "horizons"—whether invoked, posited, or created—are incapable of doing justice to the horizon of the original text. Only when the single horizon of the original author/text provides the interpretive parameters is interpretation that is faithful to the meaning of the original ancient text and responsible to its present significance possible.[29]

As a result of adopting a single horizon hermeneutics, there is a significant and meaningful place for many if not all legitimate interpretive methods. Rather than simply reverting to the theological beliefs of the church of the fourth century, or entoning a particular creed, or invoking a nebulous interpretive construct called church tradition, a single horizon hermeneutics demands focus upon the ancient text itself, with all of its interpretive challenges firmly in place, not smoothed away or otherwise mitigated by later ecclesial or theological refinement.

Church history in such a model becomes a set of examples of the history of interpretation of the biblical text, from its earliest interpreters (for example, the New Testament writers interpreting the Old Testament) to the present. Such significant interpretive moments as the development of the many early creeds are examined for their importance, not least as indicators of matters of interpretive disagreement and proposals of tentative resolution, but not as final or determinative interpretations of the Bible—especially in their paraphrastic and interpretive language that invokes non-biblical formulations. Other important interpretive moments—though ones not always recognized for their ecclesial effect—are ecclesial institutionalization and the interpretive result of transforming the Christian church from a divinely instigated and functionally arranged organism into a humanly structured and politically appointed institution. Further moments of importance are the rise of the medieval church, with its scholasticism, as well as various internal and external theological conflicts that resulted in various schisms, whether broad or narrow, external or internal. These schismatic tendencies, to which the church as a human institution has always been susceptible, again help to define issues of conflict and potential divergent understanding and even misunderstanding. I believe that these trends

---

29. A somewhat similar approach is found in Lewis, "Modern Theology and Biblical Criticism"; Lewis, *English Literature*, 32; and Lewis, *Experiment in Criticism*. See also Jackson, *Historical Criticism*, and his definition and utilization of it.

have been exacerbated within the context of institutionalized religion, which has overlayed simpler church organization with manifold ecclesial structures. The history of interpretation would not be complete without the work of the Reformations and the counter-Reformation. The Reformation itself is a multi-faceted interpretive complex, in which various theological priorities resulted from varied contemporaneous historical, political, and religious contexts. These Reformations called forth a counter-Reformation that has its own interpretive hallmarks, and which came to a hermeneutical crisis in the Second Vatican Council. In the meantime, the so-called Protestant church, which soon became less oriented to protest and more geared toward maintenance and establishment, encouraged Enlightenment thought and biblical interpretation that attempted to mediate the biblical world through its interpretive grid, straining out assumptions and results that appeared to run contrary to understanding of the modern world, even a modern world that itself was scientifically uncertain and still given to categorical fickleness. Globalization has, as a result, strained modernist biblical interpretation, because it has forced sedentary and self-secure Western interpreters to acknowledge their interpretive hegemony, while also compelling them to confront the fact that the majority world may not share its limited modernist, scientistic horizon.

Theology itself is in many ways a more idealized reflection of the historical conflicts that the church and society have undergone in the last two thousand years. There remain attempts to make systematic or dogmatic theology an entity in itself, as if theology were an a-contextual endeavor. This is still to be seen in various nominal theological positions that assert—as if the assertion were the same as revelation—the inherent rightness of one theological system over another, failing to note that each such system is conditioned by its inciting environment and the reflective thought that emerged from it—however closely tied to the Bible it may purport to be. However, much recent theology has accepted that systematic or dogmatic theology (it is not necessary to parse the difference in this article) is a final product of reflective, contextual thought, and not an instigating force in interpretation.[30] The problem is not with theology being systematic or even dogmatic (if dogmatism is understood in its best possible light), but with how the systems and dogmas are formulated and the grounds on which they are laid. Theology is a third order synthetic interpretive endeavor, drawing upon the first order conclusions of biblical interpretation, and the second order partial-synthetic results of biblical theology (including that of the New Testament and Old Testaments, or as a whole). There is an unfortunate tendency to invoke a multi-horizoned hermeneutic that includes systematic theology, in which the system has equal status with the biblical evidence and the biblical theological organization. This often results in a top-down inversion of necessary interpretive procedure. In a single horizon hermeneutics, the biblical evidence is the foundation that supports the partial-synthesis of biblical theology, which is then able to be systematized into the kinds of categories—whether they are dogmatically or philosophically formulated—of systematic theology.

Biblical interpretation involves the most important, and understandably most precarious, place within a single horizon hermeneutics. Much of the complaint against modern interpretive and exegetical procedure has revolved around how modern horizons of interpretation have led to devaluing the meaning and even foundational significance of the biblical text within the life of the modern church. There is no doubt much truth in this accusation. Some of the blame must be laid on interpretive methods that are, perhaps not necessarily in and of themselves (although some might be), biased toward embracing a minimalist interpretive agenda. These methods, which by orientation are dismissive of evidence, can then be constrained by interpreters to produce minimalist and even highly skeptical and anti-foundational conclusions. There are other interpretive methods, however, that are not inherently biased in such a way, but that are, while not theory neutral in their formulation, more maximalist in orientation and provide results that support the position and place of the biblical text. There is no doubt that there is

---

30. See, for example, Hodgson and King, *Christian Theology*; and Bloesch, *Theology of Word and Spirit*.

within the hermeneutical panoply of modern interpretation a mix of methods and interpretive attitudes that can result in a variety of interpretive results, ranging from destructive and minimalist readings to uncritical and maximalist reinscriptions. The fundamental problem, however, does not seem to be with the methods or even the interpreters, but with the hermeneutical framework itself. All of these interpretive approaches attempt to function within the two horizons hermeneutics, in which there is an attempt—by means of method and interpretive inclination—to bridge the two hermeneutical horizons by means of modern interpretive approaches. The result is bound to constrict and even distort the biblical text, because, even if the modern interpreter does not wish to subsume the biblical horizon to the modern one, the two horizon approach itself is based upon a fusion and hence a compromise of horizons.

Instead, when a single horizon hermeneutics is adopted, certain assumptions of the horizon itself are put in place. These are closely bound to the worldview of the original author, the social history and configuration of the peoples involved, the sociolinguistic contexts of the participants, the political, economic, and anthropological/sociological orientations of the active entities, and the religious beliefs and orientations of all concerned. The resulting interpretive configuration allows and even insists upon any and all available interpretive and exegetical tools to be marshaled to examine the texts within their original horizon, so long as they can function within the operative horizon of the biblical authors. Methods that do not conform to these ancient interpretive parameters, and that therefore attempt to draw the biblical text into a world foreign to itself, while they may have merit in helping us to understand the modern interpreter, can only create misleading and even possibly false interpretive conclusions of the original text. In other words, they provide answers for questions that have not been asked and in some cases cannot or possibly even should not be asked of the biblical text—if by that one is interested in understanding the text as it was called forth by the ancients, rather than as an exploration in modern interpretive legerdemain.

Conclusion

This article has attempted to offer a brief exploration of the notion of a single horizon hermeneutics. This has been a study in hermeneutics, addressing the shortcomings of the reigning hermeneutical paradigm, and proposing that another paradigm has better hermeneutical claims and interpretive possibilities. I have not addressed the questions of actual interpretation of texts. In some ways, I do not believe that I must do this, because the interpretive paradigms themselves are largely determinative for their interpretive conclusions. If one invokes the two horizon hermeneutics one may well arrive at a conclusion that is compatible with a modern understanding of the world, but in its attempt to be reflective of that world it must inevitably compromise its view of the ancient world. If my assumption is correct that interpretation of the Bible (whatever else some may think it is about) is at the very least about discerning the meaning of the ancient author/text, then a single horizon hermeneutics—while not necessarily answering all interpretive questions—provides a more reasonable, more responsible, and ultimately more satisfactory reading than other proposed methods. By this I mean it will have a better chance of actually reflecting the meaning of the author/text within its ancient context.

Bibliography

Adam, A. K. M., et al. *Reading Scripture with the Church: Toward a Hermeneutic for Theological Interpretation.* Grand Rapids: Baker, 2006.

Baird, William. *History of New Testament Research.* 2 vols. Minneapolis: Fortress, 1992.

Bedard, Stephen. Review of *The Resurrection of the Son of God*, by N. T. Wright. *JGRChJ* 5 (2008) R51–R55. Online: http://www.jgrchj.net/reviews/5.R51-R55_Bedard%20on%20Wright.pdf

Billings, J. Todd. *The Word of God for the People of God: An Entryway to the Theological Interpretation of Scripture*. Grand Rapids: Eerdmans, 2010.

Bloesch, Donald G. *A Theology of Word and Spirit: Authority and Method in Theology*. Downers Grove, IL: InterVarsity, 1992.

Bockmuehl, Markus. *Seeing the Word: Refocusing New Testament Study*. Grand Rapids: Baker, 2006.

Bonnycastle, Stephen. *In Search of Authority: An Introductory Guide to Literary Theory*. 2nd ed. Peterborough, ON: Broadview, 1996.

Brown, Colin. *Miracles and the Critical Mind*. Grand Rapids: Eerdmans, 1984.

Bultmann, Rudolf. "New Testament and Mythology." In *Kerygma and Myth: A Theological Debate*, edited by Hans Werner Bartsch, translated by Reginald H. Fuller, 1–44. London: SPCK, 1953 (1941).

Childs, Brevard S. *Introduction to the Old Testament as Scripture*. Philadelphia: Fortress, 1979.

———. *The New Testament as Canon: An Introduction*. Valley Forge, PA: Trinity Press International, 1984.

Cunningham, Valentine. *Reading after Theory*. London: Blackwell, 1992.

Donoghue, Denis. *The Practice of Reading*. New Haven: Yale University Press, 1998.

Fowl, Stephen E. *Engaging Scripture: A Model for Theological Interpretation*. Oxford: Blackwell, 1998.

———. *Theological Interpretation of Scripture*. Eugene, OR: Cascade, 2009.

———, ed. *The Theological Interpretation of Scripture: Classic and Contemporary Readings*. Oxford: Blackwell, 1997.

Gadamer, Hans-Georg. *Truth and Method*. Translated by Joel Weinsheimer and Donald G. Marshall. 2nd rev. ed. New York: Continuum, 2002.

Green, Joel B. *Practicing Theological Interpretation: Engaging Biblical Texts for Faith and Formation*. Grand Rapids: Baker, 2011.

———. *Seized by Truth: Reading the Bible as Scripture*. Nashville: Abingdon, 2007.

Hodgson, Peter C., and Robert H. King. *Christian Theology: An Introduction to Its Traditions and Tasks*. Updated ed. Minneapolis: Fortress, 1994.

Jackson, J. R. de J. *Historical Criticism and the Meaning of Texts*. London: Routledge, 1989.

Jenkins, Philip. *The New Faces of Christianity: Believing the Bible in the Global South*. Oxford: Oxford University Press, 1992.

Keener, Craig S. *Miracles: The Credibility of the New Testament Accounts*. 2 vols. Grand Rapids: Baker, 2011.

Klein, William W., et al. *Introduction to Biblical Interpretation*. 2nd ed. Dallas: Word, 2004.

Klemke, E. D. *Contemporary Analytic and Linguistic Philosophies*. Buffalo, NY: Prometheus, 1983.

Leithart, Peter J. *Defending Constantine: The Twilight of an Empire and the Dawn of Christendom.* Downers Grove, IL: InterVarsity, 2010.

Lewis, C. S. *The Discarded Image: An Introduction to Medieval and Renaissance Literature.* Cambridge: Cambridge University Press, 1964.

———. *English Literature in the Sixteenth Century, Excluding Drama.* Oxford: Oxford University Press, 1954.

———. *An Experiment in Criticism.* Cambridge: Cambridge University Press, 1961.

———. "Modern Theology and Biblical Criticism." In *Christian Reflections*, edited by Walter Hooper, 152–66. Grand Rapids: Eerdmans, 1967.

Lincona, Michael R. *The Resurrection of Jesus: A New Historiographical Approach.* Downers Grove, IL: InterVarsity, 2010.

Livingston, Paisley. *Literary Knowledge: Humanistic Inquiry and the Philosophy of Science.* Ithaca, NY: Cornell University Press, 1988.

Osborne, Grant R. *The Hermeneutical Spiral: A Comprehensive Introduction to Biblical Interpretation.* Rev. ed. Downers Grove, IL: InterVarsity, 2006.

Overman, Dean L. *A Case for the Existence of God.* Lanham, MD: Rowman and Littlefield, 2009.

Plantinga, Alvin, and Nicholas Wolterstorff, eds. *Faith and Rationality: Reason and Belief in God.* Notre Dame: University of Notre Dame Press, 1983.

Porter, Stanley E . "The Implications of New Testament Pseudonymy for a Doctrine of Scripture." In *Interdisciplinary Perspectives on the Authority of Scripture: Historical, Biblical, and Theoretical Perspectives*, edited by Carlos R. Bovell, 236–56. Eugene, OR: Pickwick, 2011.

———. "Pauline Authorship and the Pastoral Epistles: A Response to R. W. Wall's Response." *BBR* 6 (1996) 133–38.

———. "Pauline Authorship and the Pastoral Epistles: Implications for Canon." *BBR* 5 (1995) 105–23.

———. "What Difference Does Hermeneutics Make? Hermeneutical Method Applied." *Jian Dao* 34/*Pastoral Journal* 27 (July 2010) 1–50.

Porter, Stanley E., and Jason C. Robinson. *Hermeneutics: An Introduction to Interpretive Theory*. Grand Rapids: Eerdmans, 2011.

Reventlow, Henning Graf. *History of Biblical Interpretation*. Translated by Leo G. Perdue and James O. Duke. 4 vols. Atlanta: SBL, 2009–2010.

Seitz, Christopher R. *The Character of Christian Scripture: The Significance of a Two-Testament Bible*. Grand Rapids: Baker, 2011.

Sollors, Werner. *The Return of Thematic Criticism*. Cambridge, MA: Harvard University Press, 1993.

Taylor, Vincent. *The Names of Jesus*. London: Macmillan, 1962.

Thiselton, Anthony C. *New Horizons in Hermeneutics*. Grand Rapids: Zondervan, 1992.

———. *The Two Horizons: New Testament Hermeneutics and Philosophical Description with Special Reference to Heidegger, Bultmann, Gadamer, and Wittgenstein.* Grand Rapids: Eerdmans, 1980.

Treier, Daniel J. *Introducing Theological Interpretation of Scripture: Recovering a Christian Practice.* Grand Rapids: Baker, 2008.

Vanhoozer, Kevin J., ed. *Dictionary for Theological Interpretation of the Bible.* Grand Rapids: Baker, 2005.

———. *The Drama of Doctrine: A Canonical Linguistic Approach to Christian Theology.* Louisville: Westminster John Knox, 2005.

———. *Is There a Meaning in This Text? The Bible, the Reader and the Morality of Literary Knowledge.* Grand Rapids: Zondervan, 1998.

Wall, Robert W. "Pauline Authorship and the Pastoral Epistles: A Response to S. E. Porter." *BBR* 5 (1995) 125–28.

Wall, Robert W., and Eugene E. Lemcio. *The New Testament as Canon: A Reader in Canonical Criticism.* JSNTSup 76. Sheffield: JSOT Press, 1992.

Watson, Francis. *Text and Truth: Redefining Biblical Theology.* Edinburgh: T. & T. Clark, 1997.

———. *Text, Church, and World: Biblical Interpretation in Theological Perspective.* Grand Rapids: Eerdmans, 1994.

Wright, N. T. *The Resurrection of the Son of God.* London: SPCK, 2003.

CREATION, PROGRESS, AND CALLING:
GENESIS 1–11 AS SOCIAL COMMENTARY*

Paul S. Evans
McMaster Divinity College

"Against the whole rushing stream of contemporary life,
the individual feels himself rather powerless."
— James Truslow Adams (1931)

"Science Finds, Industry Applies, Man Conforms."
— Motto of the 1933 World's Fair

Introduction

The two quotations that begin this essay, though both dating to around 80 years ago, could read as if they were written recently. Adams's words could easily express the feelings of one living in the twenty-first century and the motto of the 1933 World's Fair could many times describe the way technology is applied in our modern context. Is there nothing new under the sun? Genesis is an ancient book. However, it is also a surprisingly modern book in many ways. The interpretation of Genesis 1–11 continues to be a controversial issue for all sorts of people. Whether one is a theological "liberal" or "conservative," how one reads these chapters of the Bible is often viewed as a *shibboleth* of orthodoxy.[1] Among the controversies surrounding the interpretation

---

* An earlier version of this essay was presented in McMaster University's Albert Lager Lecture Series (McMaster Alumni Association), Hamilton, ON, 11 May 11 2011. As well, much of its content was delivered in the form of a sermon in the Nathaniel H. Parker Chapel of McMaster Divinity College on 21 September, 2011.

1. As Watts, "Making Sense," 2, aptly puts it, "hold the 'wrong' view and one is either a dupe of secular critical theory or a troglodyte literalist."

of Genesis 1–11, questions of its relation to the conclusions of modern science are significant. Was the world created in seven literal days? What was the process of creation? Was there a global flood? The descriptions of the first human couple and the pronouncements rendered against them subsequent to their disobedience in the garden continue to be controversial. What are the implications for relationships between the genders? What do these narratives say about the establishment of so-called patriarchy? The early chapters of Genesis have also been the crucible for source criticism and the theories that different documentary sources were combined to form the book of Genesis and the entire Pentateuch. Often it is in these first chapters of Genesis where the isolation of putative sources appears most compelling (specifically identifying sources based on choice of a "divine name" used in each passage).[2]

Despite these well-known issues, this article is not meant to focus specifically on scientific or gender issues, nor will it offer a fresh source critical analysis of any kind. In my opinion such controversial issues have sometimes distracted readers from vital aspects of the theological message of these foundational chapters in the Bible. Therefore, in this essay I intend to examine these chapters "as is," in their final form, taking into account their current literary context (as part of the book of Genesis) and their ancient historical context (as a creation story among many in the ancient Near East). My aim here is to discern how Genesis 1–11 functioned as social commentary in its day, and to uncover its continued relevance for today.

---

2. As is well known, some of the earliest source critical delineations were based on whether a passage used "Elohim" or "Yahweh," as it was thought that the exclusive use of one or the other in a passage was evidence for a source being used that preferred one divine name (or only knew of the one divine name). The literature on such source critical question in the Pentateuch is voluminous and discussions can be found in any handbook on Old Testament criticism or Old Testament introduction. Cf. Blenkinsopp, *Pentateuch*, and Alexander, *Paradise*.

Genesis 1–11 as a Literary Unit

Literarily, Genesis 1–11 can be understood as a distinct literary unit within the book of Genesis. Commentators usually divide the book into two distinct sections, chapters 1–11 and 12–50. The first section focuses on world history and covers a span of thousands of years, while the second section focuses only on the history of Israel (particularly a few men from whom Israel descends) and covers only a couple of hundred years. Furthermore, Genesis 1–11 has a clear focus on "firsts" and contains many etiological narratives—explaining the origins of things. The origins of worship, cities, technology, population, wine making, and empire building, are all referred to in its chapters.[3] Further setting it off from what follows is the radical decline in ages in the Patriarchal narratives that follow these chapters. While in Genesis 1–11 several people live to over nine hundred years (with Methuselah living to 969) and many live for over six centuries, even the central characters in the following narratives live brief lives by comparison (Abraham lives to only 175 years of age). Finally, the stories in Genesis 1–11 often have characters and places with symbolic names. The first man is named Adam, which is the Hebrew word for "humankind"; his wife is named Havvah (Eve) or "lifer" (i.e., the life giving one); they give birth to a son named "Habel" (Abel), which is Hebrew for "vanity," or "vapor" (and Abel's life is brief and disappears like a vapor); Eden is a pun on the Hebrew word for "pleasure" or "delight";[4] the name of Noah's son, Shem, is identical to the Hebrew word for "name," and Abraham, the one whose name (*shem*) God makes great (Gen 12:2), is a descendent of the line of Shem.

In sum, all of these considerations provide a compelling rationale for viewing Genesis 1–11 as a distinct literary unit. Therefore, in what follows I will focus on the opening eleven chapters of the book, though not ignoring their context in the book of Genesis as a whole.

---

3. Blenkinsopp, *Creation*, 2.
4. Westermann, *Genesis 1–11*, 210; Blenkinsopp, *Creation*, 62.

Reading Genesis 1–11 in Its Cultural Context

Noting the cultural context of a piece of literature aids in interpretation. Only in this way can one know what the contemporary issues were at the time a piece of literature was written. Though Genesis is Holy Scripture, good interpretation needs to take into account its cultural context in order to hear the Word more clearly. This brings us to the issue of ancient Near Eastern parallel texts that were prevalent in Genesis's cultural context.

Ancient Near Eastern Parallels

In order to better discern the original message of Genesis 1–11 it is important to read it in the context of its ancient Near Eastern environment. As is well known, in the 1800s cuneiform tablets from ancient Mesopotamia were discovered and deciphered and it quickly became clear that these ancient Near Eastern texts had many significant parallels with Genesis. For example, the poem of Gilgamesh, the Epic of Atrahasis, and the Sumerian flood tablet all show remarkable similarities to Genesis, particularly to the Flood narrative in chapters 6–9.[5] Some of the most important parallels are as follows:

> Divine decision to destroy humankind
> Warning to the flood hero
> Command to build the ark
> The hero's obedience
> Command to enter
> Entry into the ark
> Closing the door of the ark
> Description of the flood
> Destruction of life
> End of rain
> Ark grounding on mountain
> The hero opens a window
> Birds' reconnaissance
> Exit from the Ark

---

5. For English translations of these texts, see Dalley, *Myths*.

Sacrifices offered after leaving the ark
Divine smelling of sacrifice
Blessing on the flood hero[6]

Due to these and other striking parallels most scholars began to assume that the author of Genesis was familiar with Mesopotamian mythological traditions very similar to the form in which we know them. In fact, since the discovery of these ancient Near Eastern parallels, many scholars have suggested that Genesis actually directly borrowed from these ancient Near Eastern texts.[7] Others have suggested that the plot of Genesis 1–11 as a whole was taken over from one or more of these ancient texts.[8] What is more, these ancient Mesopotamian texts date to the third millennium BC—before the time of Moses.[9]

Of course, there were many occasions in Israel's history when Israel could have learned of these myths. Abraham is said to come from Mesopotamia (Genesis 11), Israel was an ally of Babylon in the days of Hezekiah (2 Kings 20), and of course Judah itself was exiled to Babylon for a generation.[10]

However, despite the similarities, the differences between the Genesis text and these ancient Near Eastern texts are significant. In fact, it could be argued that they are too different to conclude that Genesis borrowed directly from these texts. Of course, it is possible that both the biblical and non-biblical texts reflect reliance on a common tradition. But whether Genesis borrowed from these texts or drew on a common tradition, it seems clear that Genesis made use of textual or oral traditions prevalent in the culture in which its author lived. As Blenkinsopp writes, the author did "what all competent authors do, namely, incorporating

---

6. This list is slightly paraphrased from Wenham's list of common elements between biblical and non-biblical flood accounts. Cf. Wenham, *Genesis 1–15*, 163–64.

7. Heidel, *Babylonian Genesis*, 82.

8. So Wenham, *Genesis 1–15*.

9. This is so no matter which date for the Exodus is chosen, a fifteenth century date (ca. 1446 BC) or a thirteenth century date (ca. 1266 BC).

10. If Genesis was completed during this time of exile in Babylon (as scholarly orthodoxy asserts) the author's knowledge of Mesopotamian traditions is easily explained.

ideas, traditions, motifs from the great store present in the cultural memory of the society of which he was a part."[11] As a believer in the full inspiration of Scripture, I would add that the author did so as guided by the Spirit.

In light of the existence of other ancient stories of the creation and flood etc. that were part of the cultural heritage of the ancient Near East, it is important for the reader of Genesis to gain some familiarity with them in order to get a sense of the issues that were current in that ancient culture and see how they talked about such things.[12] As Watts asserts, "we are not talking about borrowing or dependence but rather about the use of common motifs and ideas to deal with common concerns."[13]

Given that these Genesis narratives purposefully drew on and responded to literary and oral traditions from their ancient cultural environment, we may read Genesis against their backdrop and compare and contrast them, in order to see how their views agreed or disagreed with their neighbors. As we will see, such a reading brings into relief several important themes that actually become "central affirmations of the Christian faith."[14]

Themes in Genesis 1–11

God as Sole Creator

One of the consistent features of ancient Near Eastern creation stories is the depiction of the process of creation taking place only after the defeat of malevolent forces that resist creation. In Enuma Elish, the goddess Tiamat is a huge dragon of chaotic water that resists order.[15] The hero-god Marduk, with the aid of some other gods, defeats her and uses her carcass to create the cosmos. Marduk uses half of her carcass for the firmament/the heavens to keep the waters above separate from below, and half her carcass to create the dry land where life can exist.

---

11. Blenkinsopp, *Creation*, 56.
12. Watts, "Making Sense," 2.
13. Ibid.
14. Wenham, *Genesis 1–15*, 221.
15. Foster, "Epic of Creation."

The name of the chaos dragon in Enuma Elish, "Tiamat," is very similar to the Hebrew word for the deep/deep water (*tehôm*), which is used in Gen 1:2.[16] Tiamat is a salt water deity and representative of the ocean, so the connection between Tiamat and the deep water is intriguing as both Tiamat and *tehôm* in Gen 2:1 refer to the "primeval" water. This is not to say that Genesis depends on Enuma Elish,[17] but the use of the word *tehôm* in this context would have recalled to the ancient reader the widely known story/stories that contained the motif of a battle with the sea/sea dragon in the context of creation.[18]

As I mentioned, the goddess Tiamat is a dragon. In Hebrew, the word for dragon is *tannîn* (see. Isa 27:1; 51:9; Ps 74:13; Job 7:12). What is significant for our purposes is that the *tannîn* (dragon) also appears in Genesis 1. In Gen 1:21 we read:

> And God created the great sea dragons (*tannîn*) and every living creature that creeps, of every kind, which the waters produced in swarms, and every winged bird of every kind. And God saw that this was good.[19]

In other words, Genesis 1, like those ancient Near Eastern parallel texts, mentions a dragon in the creation account.

---

16. Ever since Gunkel's famous study, *Schöpfung*, many scholars have argued that the water dragon goddess Tiamat from Enuma Elish was the mythological background to the Hebrew *tehôm* (deep) in Gen 1:2. However, Tsumura, *Earth and the Waters*, 45–52, has convincingly shown that the Hebrew *tehôm* is not derived from Tiamat but that **tiham* was a common Semitic term referring to the ocean.

17. As Lambert, "A New Look," 103, has argued, "the watery beginning of Genesis in itself is no evidence of Mesopotamian influence."

18. Kapelrud, "Mythological Features," 183, has suggested that *tehôm* is an allusion to Tiamat but that the intention of the writer of Genesis 1 was "not to use the Babylonian myth, but to indicate through his allusions that he knew it, and disregarded its content."

19. All translations of Scripture in this essay are my own. Some translations translate *tannîn* in Gen 1:21 as "sea monsters" (e.g., NRSV, JPS, ASV). Other versions (e.g., CEB, NLT, NIV) translate this word as "sea creatures" or "sea animals" in Gen 1:21, despite the fact that these same translations render the word as either dragon, serpent, or monster elsewhere. Cf. Isa 27:1; 51:9; Ps 74:13; Job 7:12.

When we are armed with this knowledge of the ancient context of creation accounts, the purpose of Genesis 1 becomes clearer. In Gen 1:2, we see the deep (*tehôm*) in existence before creation is ordered. However, contrary to ancient Near Eastern myths, the deep is simply water—not an enemy god (Tiamat). There is no conflict necessary to create. There are no other gods for Yahweh to fight in order to create. The dragon (*tannîn*) is referenced, but in Genesis 1 it is not a malevolent deity but merely one of the creatures God made. In other words, in Genesis 1 monotheism is declared. Far from creation in the context of other gods, only one God is present. Further, instead of the context of a victorious battle, God creates by merely speaking.[20]

This polemic against the prevailing polytheistic culture of the day can be seen further in the way Gen 1:16 refers to the sun and moon as simply the "greater light" and the "lesser light."[21] This reticence to explicitly mention the sun (*shamesh*) and moon (*yareah*) was likely because in Canaan and Mesopotamia, the name of the sun god was Shamesh and the name of the moon god was Yareah. In other words, the names of these gods were the same as the name of the heavenly bodies they represented.[22] The worship of the sun and moon was ubiquitous in the ancient Near East, and Israel itself struggled with this vice.[23] Refusing to use their names in Gen 1:16 was due to the polemic against polytheism—they are not gods at all. Further denigrating the divine

---

20. In fact, as Tsumura, "Genesis and Ancient Near Eastern Stories," 31, points out, this "creation by divine fiat in Genesis is unique in the ancient Near East."

21. Unfortunately, the NLT uses the words "sun" and "moon" in its translation, even though they are not present in the original Hebrew text. This of course communicates what "lights" are referred to very clearly but it misses the intentional omission of their proper names that was intended to denigrate their commonly perceived status as gods.

22. Shamash (Akkadian Šamaš, "Sun") was the name of the sun god in the Akkadian, Assyrian, and Babylonian pantheons. Similarly, Yareah is the Canaanite name of the moon god. He is mentioned in Ugaritic texts, though he is not as well known as Shamesh.

23. Even in Israel, the worship of the sun had to be fought against. See Josiah's efforts in 2 Kgs 23–24. Cf. Taylor, *Yahweh and the Sun*.

status of the sun, God creates light without the sun. Light is created on the first day, while the sun is not created until the fourth day.[24]

In sum, the creation account in Genesis 1 does not borrow directly from other ancient Near Eastern creation accounts.[25] But it does appear to purposefully allude to them in order to refute their theology.[26] There is only one God and he created the universe by speaking it into existence, not by defeating the forces of divine evil or chaos. These assertions are primary theological grounds for the faith. God is God alone, there is no other. Creation is his doing and its existence owes to his creativity alone and not the exigency of malevolent forces out of which creation was made.[27] This brings up the issue of the nature of creation.

The Goodness of Creation
Far from being created from the carcass of a malevolent deity or sea-dragon, creation is viewed as good. There is no trace of residual evil owing to its origins in an evil divine cadaver. Seven times in Genesis 1 the Creator declares that creation is nothing less than good (Gen 1:4, 10, 12, 18, 21, 25, 31). In fact, on the final day he declares that it is "very good" (Gen 1:31). Genesis does not hold to a dualistic worldview with the notion of the "goodness" of the spiritual and the "evilness" of the physical. Genesis does not advocate a pie in the sky theology, but an earthy reality. The physical is not viewed as a temporary vice that must be tolerated until the goodness of the spirit is released from its physical prison. Genesis 1 states categorically that God

---

24. The light as the first thing created is unique in ancient Near Eastern texts. Cf. Tsumura, "Genesis and Ancient Near Eastern Stories," 31.

25. As Lambert, "A New Look," 105, has maintained, there is "no evidence of Hebrew borrowing from Babylon." As Tsumura, "Genesis and Ancient Near Eastern Stories," 32, concludes, "It is not correct to say that 'Enuma Elish' was adopted and adapted by the Israelites to produce the Genesis stories."

26. So Hasel, "Polemic Nature."

27. Wenham, *Genesis 1–15*, l, suggests that "Because as Christians we tend to assume these points in our theology, we often fail to recognize the striking originality of the message of Genesis 1–11 and concentrate on subsidiary points that may well be of less moment."

created physical things "good." This has implications regarding what kind of attitude toward creation we should have. That physical creation is deeply valued has environmental implications, which we will explore below.

However, as "good" as creation was at the beginning, it is not said to be "perfect." The Hebrew word frequently translated as "perfect" (תם) means "complete" or "full."[28] Though God rested from his work on the seventh day (Gen 2:3), because his work was finished, creation was not at that point deemed "perfect" or "complete." That is, creation is not described as in a flawless state that had no possibility of improvement or further development. According to Genesis, the pre-sin world was not a utopia with only ideal situations, and devoid of work and pain. Even in the pre-sin world, God stated that the first man's situation was "not good" (Gen 2:18) until he was given a suitable partner in his wife.[29]

Pain was a reality in the pre-sin world as is made clear by the pronouncement on the woman after the Fall, which speaks of an "increase" in pain due to sin, not the introduction of pain (Gen 3:16). As well, work was clearly in view as God placed the first man in the garden to "work" and "keep/guard" it (Gen 2:15). The fact that the original state of creation was not perfect leaves room for human technological development, as we will see below.

The necessity for the development of creation is clearly referenced in Gen 2:5 where it states that humans were needed to "work the earth" (לעבד את־האדמה) in order for vegetation to grow. Clearly the earth had not reached its potential and in order to do so, it needed human involvement. This necessity for development can be further seen in God's commission in Gen 1:28 for humans to "subdue" (כבש) the earth, suggesting that creation from the beginning was "wild," and that some coercion on the part of humans was necessary. It further implies that this "subduing" would change and develop creation over time. Creation was not supposed to be a static reality, but was created with

---

28. Brown, Driver, and Briggs, *Hebrew and English Lexicon*, 1070.
29. Fretheim, *Creation Untamed*, 13.

potential for becoming much more than its original state. As Fretheim writes:

> Genesis does not present the creation as a finished product, wrapped up with a big red bow and handed over to the creatures to keep it exactly as originally created. It is not a onetime production. Indeed, for the creation to stay just as God originally created it would constitute a failure of the divine design. From God's perspective, the world needs work; development and change are what God intends for it, and God enlists human beings (and other creatures) to that end.[30]

To sum up, physical things matter (no pun intended). They are good. However, they are not perfect. God has ordained humanity to facilitate creation in developing its fullest possible potential.[31]

At this point it is necessary to consider the implications of the mandate in Genesis 1 for humanity to have "dominion" and "subdue" the earth. Lest some think that this command encourages the idea that humans have carte blanche when it comes to how they might treat creation, a deeper investigation of the two Hebrew words behind the terms "take dominion" (רדה) and "subdue" (כבשׁ) will be helpful.

This verb "take dominion" (רדה) is used twenty-two times in the Old Testament and in every instance outside of Genesis 1 it is used in the context of humans "ruling" over humans.[32] Most significantly, when the verb is used, it is generally speaking about authority being exercised in a humane manner (e.g., Lev 25:43; Ezek 34:4).[33] Thus, the verb does not connote harshness or brutality in any way.[34]

---

30. Fretheim, *Creation Untamed*, 14.
31. Ibid., 13.
32. Only in Gen 1:26, 28 is it used of ruling non-human creatures or entities.
33. Blenkinsopp, *Creation*, 26.
34. When this is expressed in the Old Testament, descriptors are attached to the verb to indicate a harsh manner of "ruling." E.g., Lev 25:46 speaks of a "ruthless" rule (לא־תרדה בו בפרך); Isa 14:6 speaks of a "rule in fury/anger" (רדה באף); and Ezek 34:4 of a "brutal/harsh" rule (אתם ובפרך רדיתם).

The verb "subdue" (כבשׁ) is found fifteen times in the Old Testament and, like "take dominion" (רדה), it is used only in the context of humans "subduing" other humans.[35] However, the word is clearly used of coercive behavior that is not always in the best interest of the one "subdued."[36] Even so, the literary context of the use of this verb must be taken into account before we can conclude that it has a negative connotation in Gen 1:28. Fretheim writes:

> the verb [כבשׁ] is here used in a pre-sin context, before any negative effects that sin has brought, and apparently no enemies are in view. Given its use in a pre-sin context, one should be careful not simply to transfer the usage of the verb for post-sin human activity to an understanding of this word here.[37]

In light of this literary context, the terms "take dominion" and "subdue" must be read in light of the role that humans play in God's creation in a pre-sin environment. What exactly is the role of humankind?

The Role of Humankind

The role of humankind envisioned by Genesis 1 is most clearly appreciated if read in light of both its ancient cultural environment and its current literary context in the opening chapters of Genesis. In ancient Near Eastern creation texts, humans are actually created to be slave labor for the gods. In fact, this idea was widespread in that ancient culture.[38] For example, in the epic of Atrahasis, the gods created people to do the work of the lower gods (basically farm labor and the digging of canals) in order to feed the gods through sacrifices. Look at the following quotation from the beginning of the Atrahasis epic:

---

35. Though it is used of the "land" several times (e.g., Num 32:22, 29; Josh 18:1) the context makes clear that it is referring to the humans who control the land and not the land itself. Cf. Fretheim, *Creation Untamed*, 14 n. 12.
36. Cf. Esth 7:8; Neh 5:5.
37. Fretheim, *Creation Untamed*, 14.
38. As Bird, "Male and Female," 345, has observed, the idea that humans were "created to relieve the gods of hard labour by supplying them with food and drink was standard among both Sumerians and Babylonians."

> Great indeed was the drudgery of the gods, the forced labor was heavy, the misery too much: The seven great Anunna-gods were burdening the Igigi-gods with forced labor.[39]

The gods then created humans to remedy the situation. After this accomplishment one of the great high gods then boasted that by creating humans "I have done away with your heavy forced labor, I have imposed your drudgery on humans . . . bestowed clamor upon humankind."[40]

Read against this background, Genesis's view of humanity is striking. Contrary to ancient Near Eastern texts, which state that humans were to provide food (sacrifices) for the gods, in Genesis God provides food for humans (Gen 1:29–30; 2:9, 15). What is more, not once does God speak of humans as being meant to function in any way to provide for God. In fact, God does not even speak of humans owing him service, allegiance, or a debt of any sort. True, there is one parameter set on them in Genesis 2—abstaining from eating from the tree of knowledge—but other than that it appears that they are given the freedom to work out for themselves what it is they will do. God does not even say ". . . but worship me." This is striking in light of later conceptions of the meaning of life as to continually worship God, or to serve him more and more. As Moltmann writes, "God does not create merely by calling something into existence, or by setting something afoot. In a more profound sense he 'creates' by letting-be, by making room, and by withdrawing himself."[41]

Strikingly, Genesis asserts that humans are created in God's image. While there has been tremendous debate over what exactly this means, it is clearly a radical departure from the anthropology of the contemporary ancient Near Eastern cultural and philosophical environment. For example, in ancient Egypt, only kings are the image of God. In ancient Mesopotamia, the king is the god's "icon, representative and viceregent."[42] Other than kings, only an idol is said to be the image of God. The idea

---

39. This is a slight paraphrase of Foster, "Atra-Hasis."
40. Ibid.
41. Moltmann, *God in Creation*, 88.
42. Blenkinsopp, *Creation*, 26.

that all men were in the image of God would have been counter-cultural. Of course, Genesis goes further than this. Genesis 1:27 makes it is very clear that all *humans*—both men and women—are created in God's image. It boldly states:

> And God created humans in his image
> in the image of God he created them
> male and female he created them.[43]

Given the common connection in the ancient Near East between kings and the image of God, Genesis referring to all humans as being in God's image connotes the royalty of all.[44] In fact, when God says that humans are to "have dominion" (רדה) over all the creatures of the earth (Gen 1:26, 28), this is royal language.[45] Kings and queens have dominion. However, as noted above, the dominion implied in Genesis 1 should not be quickly equated with the type of dominion exercised by monarchs in human history. Instead, in the pre-Fall context of Genesis 1, we should understand this dominion to be characterized by the dominion that God exercises. It is what the true king, God, does that should be the model for human regency over creation. The dominion of humankind over the earth should be expressed in nurturing, care, and protection—not exploitation (though the latter commonly has characterized the reign of human monarchs).[46]

Furthermore, Gen 1:28 declares that all humans are God-blessed and they are told to "increase in number" and fill the earth. First, it is important to read this in light of the literary context where it is part of the blessing, not a chore or a burden

---

43. The claim that all humans are in God's image was wildly radical as the ancient world was even more "patriarchal" or "andro-centric" than we are today. This concept was revolutionary with the potential to subvert the very structures on which the ancient societies were based.

44. As Clines, *Theme of the Pentateuch*, 80–85, has observed, in the ancient Near East the king is "the image of the god . . . [and] the image of the god is associated very closely with rulerhood."

45. As Bird, "Male and Female," 341, has asserted, the image of God in Genesis 1 is "a royal designation, the precondition or requisite for rule."

46. Fretheim, *Creation Untamed*, 34.

placed on humans.[47] Second, reading it in light of the contemporary ancient Near Eastern culture again reveals the counter-cultural character of Genesis more clearly. In ancient Sumerian and Babylonian accounts of the flood, the reason the gods sent the flood to destroy life on the earth was because humans had increased in number and had become noisy. Again, a passage from Atrahasis makes this clear:

> Twelve hundred years had not yet passed when . . . the peoples multiplied. The land was bellowing like a bull, the gods got disturbed with their uproar. Enlil [a god] heard their noise and addressed the great gods: The noise of humankind has become too intense for me, with their uproar I am deprived of sleep.[48]

Clearly, the increasing population of humans is seen in a negative light. However, contrary to this perspective, Genesis sees procreation as part of the blessing. Furthermore, the literary context of Gen 1:27–28 suggests that it is an important aspect to being created in the image of God.[49] This is seen in Gen 5:3:

> When Adam had lived 130 years, he had a son in his own likeness, in his own image; and he called his name Seth.

Here Adam's son, Seth, is said to be in the image of his father, who, of course, is in the image of God (Gen 5:1). Thus, the perpetuation of the image is accomplished through procreation. As

---

47. Based on translations of the word "increase" (רבה) as "multiply," some have interpreted this as a command that must be religiously followed (in order for a couple to multiply, they must have at least four children). However, this interpretation is problematic. First, the imperatives here "be fruitful and increase" do not seem to function as "commands." As Walton, *Genesis*, 375, has commented "not all imperative forms can or should be construed as commands (not much different from English in that regard)." When God told them to be fruitful and multiply, that was part of the blessing, not an obligation. Really what it is saying is "have sex"—a command that humans have continued to follow religiously to this day.

48. Arnold and Beyer, *Readings from the Ancient Near East*, 26.

49. Bird, "Male and Female," 351, suggests that the command to "be fruitful and multiply," intends a polemic against fertility cults because "the power of created life to replenish itself is a power given to each species at its creation . . . not dependent upon subsequent rites for its effect."

Fretheim has concluded: "inasmuch as human beings are created in the image of a Creator God, they themselves must be understood as creators as well."[50] Like God before them they can create new life.

Further emphasis on the importance of humanity can be seen in how human activity is presented as essential to the further development of God's creation. As we have seen, Genesis 2 begins by noting that without humans, the Garden of Eden could not grow (Gen 2:5). Furthermore, the first human is enlisted to name God's creatures (Gen 2:19–20), a role analogous to God's actions in the naming of created things in Genesis 1 (cf. Gen 1:5, 8, 10). This is striking, as the naming of something created is part of the creative process, yet in Genesis 2 God shares this with humans. Furthermore, this naming seems to have ongoing significance and is not presented as simply a temporary experiment. Genesis 2:19 states, "whatever the man called a living creature, *that was its name.*" That is, the first human's decision on what to name the animal mattered and had ongoing ramifications. As Fretheim asserts, "God has established a relationship with human beings such that their decisions about developments in creation truly count."[51]

In sum, Genesis presents humans as the image of God, God's vice-regents over the earth, who partner with God in creative acts (naming creatures), who are creators themselves (procreation), who are to exercise God-like royal dominion over the world, whose role is essential in the further development of creation and whose decisions truly count and have ongoing ramifications for creation itself.[52]

Theological implications. A biblical anthropology must take this into account when reflecting on the role of Christians today. Clearly, human life is sacred. Genesis 9:6 forbids the murder of

50. Fretheim, *Creation Untamed*, 31–32.
51. Ibid., 36.
52. As Westermann, *Genesis 1–11*, 343, writes, "The Old Testament . . . sees progress and development in the meaning of the commission that God gave his people to work on earth and bases it on the effectiveness of God's blessing."

humans explicitly on the basis that they are in God's image. Since the image of God is said to be in all people and in both genders, racism and sexism are necessarily barred on this ground as well.

A biblical cosmology must also be shaped by the perspectives of the creation accounts in Genesis 1–2. Obviously these perspectives are relevant to the realities of environmental concerns and the challenges facing humanity in the twenty-first century. The talk of humans having dominion clearly does not defend the right of humans to destroy God's good creation. God values his creation (it is "very good") and partners with it in many ways (the earth and seas participate in the bringing forth of other new creations).[53] Though humans have dominion over creation, this dominion is to be modeled on the dominion of God, who deeply values his creation and does not selfishly manipulate it for his own ends. As we have seen, creation is given freedom to be what it will be.

The fact that human decisions truly count speaks to both negative and positive effects of human decisions on the environment itself. Human actions can either aid or damage creation. This realization really is a biblical mandate for taking care of the environment. As Francis Watson writes, "Human acts which treat the nonhuman creation simply as the sphere of use-value or market-value, refusing the acknowledgment of its autonomous goodness, are acts of terrorism in direct opposition to the intention of the creator."[54] In sum, creation is good and it is humanity's responsibility to care for it. It is not something to be abused or destroyed. As God cares for his creation, we, the image of God, should follow suit.

---

53. E.g., even in Genesis 1, God partners with creation in creating new creatures. In Gen 1:11 the earth is called to "bring forth" plants and then in Gen 1:12 it says that "the earth brought vegetation." Clearly the earth is participating in bringing forth new creatures. (cf. similarly Gen 1:20, 24). As Fretheim, *Creation Untamed*, 28, writes, this "demonstrates the immense value of nonhuman creatures for God in that God involves them in the creation of still further creatures. Without the help of these nonhuman beings, God's creation would not live up to its potential of becoming."

54. Watson, *Text, Church*, 146–47.

On the other hand, the attitude that privileges the environment over humans themselves does not find grounding here. Creation is *not* divine. Neither are humans, but they are close—"a little less" than God (Ps 8:5). Humanity is central to God's plan for creation. Contrary to ancient Near Eastern anthropology, "far from being a by-product of or a solution to problems in the world of the gods, a sort of afterthought, humanity is at the centre of things, blessed by God and declared to be really good."[55] Creation is not above humanity. Further, environmental concerns should not be above humane concerns. Though creation must be cared for and not abused, humans do need to "subdue" it. There is a *wildness* to creation that humans must, at times, tame in order for creation to reach its fullest potential. Taming creation and improving quality of life leads to developments in technology, which we will discuss below. But first, this unbridled optimism of Genesis 1–2 is quickly tempered by developments in the very next chapter (Genesis 3).

The Existence of Evil: A World Gone Awry
Tempering the optimism of a creation declared good and humans said to be in the image of the divine, is the emphasis in Genesis that things have gone wrong. In fact, one of the main themes in Genesis 1–11 is how evil infiltrated this "very good" creation.[56] Throughout these chapters, several etiological narratives emphasize the spread of evil in the world. In the Garden story (Genesis 3) we see humans striving to be gods and disregarding divine commandments in the process. Another etiological narrative follows in Genesis 4, in the story of Cain and Abel and the first murder, where "sin" is mentioned for the first time.[57] Later in the same chapter, this violence is exacerbated as Lamech boasts that he has outdone the violence of Cain in murdering a

---

55. Blenkinsopp, *Creation*, 29.
56. Ibid., 186, takes this to be one of the central themes of Genesis 1–11.
57. The plot of this narrative parallels the Garden story in many ways. Instead of the snake, "sin" is said to be crouching waiting to pounce on Cain. Just as the first humans were not put to death as promised, so Cain did not undergo the death threatened. Cf. Blenkinsopp, *Creation*, 94–95.

youth (4:23).⁵⁸ Far from the later principle of *lex talionis* ("an eye for an eye and a tooth for a tooth"), calling for the punishment to fit the crime, Lamech claims to have slaughtered a youth for a mere bruise. Genesis 6 further explains the depraved state that humanity has devolved into with the short and ambiguous narrative concerning intermarriage between the sons of god and the daughters of men (Gen 6:1–4). Subsequently, God laments that all of humanity has become incorrigibly wicked with evil imaginations (Gen 6:5). The sinfulness of humanity is then met with judgment by God in the form of a devastating flood (Genesis 6–9). Speaking to its cultural environment, Genesis accents the evil of human violence and God's radical condemnation of the same.

This pessimistic outlook of Genesis on the human condition as sinful and the presentation of God as a just and moral deity was countercultural in its day. Whereas, as we have seen, in ancient Near Eastern flood texts, the flood was sent due to the petty complaints of the gods, who were annoyed by the noise of a growing human population, in Genesis the flood was sent due to the violence and evil of humankind. This spread of violence and moral depravity is countered by the presentation of a God who opposes such iniquity and is a moral deity. While the flood hero in Mesopotamian texts only survives due to the trickery of one of the gods (and to the disappointment and chagrin of the most powerful god, Enlil) in Genesis Noah is saved due to God's grace/mercy (חן, Gen 6:8). Furthermore, Noah's righteous character is emphasized (Gen 6:9).⁵⁹ The narrative ends with

---

58. The word translated "youth" (ילד) usually is translated "child," but in this instance it is parallel to "man" (איש), so, it is probably not a child that is intended. The boast could be taken as referring to the killing of a man and a child, but the parallelism militates against this view. Wenham, *Genesis 1–15*, 114, points out that ילד covers a range of ages and includes young adults "as opposed to old men whose strength has declined."

59. Contra Wenham, *Genesis 1–15*, xlix, who asserts that "Noah was saved because he was righteous, a point demonstrated by his behavior throughout the flood." Nowhere does God say he is saving Noah due to his righteousness, but instead states that "Noah found grace in the eyes of YHWH" (Gen 6:8). The next verse does accent Noah's righteous character in contradistinction to the

God vowing never again to bring such a flood on the earth, covenanting with humans, and reaffirming the blessing, once again saying, "Be fruitful and increase, and fill the earth" (Gen 9:1). This promise is made in spite of God's realization that humans remain in their utterly sinful state with the "intents of the human heart being evil from his youth" (Gen 8:21).

The spread of sin tempers the optimism of the creation accounts and, in turn, diminishes the capability for creation to reach its potential. However, as sin spreads, so does God's mercy as each transgression is met with a mitigation of the punishment and grace.[60] But the myth of progress is given little credence. Genesis does not present human rationality and goodness as capable of conquering the violence and sin that has spread so rapidly in corrupting what was deemed "very good." However, Genesis clearly presents a deity who cares deeply for his creation and continues to give his creatures second chances and reiterates his blessing on them despite continued wickedness (Gen 8:21).

The Rise of Technology
Even following the infiltration of evil into God's good creation, the blessings continue to be worked out as humans "multiply" as noted in the genealogies of Genesis 4–5. Furthermore, humans begin to fulfill their role in developing the earth. Genesis 4 says that Cain worked the ground (one of the expressed purposes of humans in Genesis 2). Along these same lines, in the genealogy in Genesis 4, the descendents of Cain are presented as technological and cultural innovators.[61] Seven of Cain's descendents are credited with the origins of city building (4:17),[62] the use of tents

---

contemporaneous generation, but it does not connect this with explaining God's favor.
    60. Clines, *Theme of the Pentateuch*, 70–80.
    61. Blenkinsopp, *Creation*, 87.
    62. There is some ambiguity regarding who builds the first city in Genesis 4—Cain or his son Enoch. The Hebrew could be read either way. Some scholars suggest it is Enoch who builds the city since it says he named it after his son (Gen 4:17). Enoch's son is Irad, a name strikingly similar to the name Eridu, which is the name of the first city ever built according to many different ancient Mesopotamian sources.

(4:20), music (4:21) and metal-working (4:22). From a modern perspective, these technologies may not seem innovative, but at the time they were real advances that aided in the flourishing of human life. Furthermore, in the present literary context up to this point these innovative technologies are presented in a positive light.[63] Some interpreters have suggested that since they are part of the line of Cain the book of Genesis is probably viewing technology in a negative light from the outset.[64] However, it seems clear that these technologies are *not* suspect on their own. For example, in the Genesis narratives, Israel's patriarchs lived in tents, their eponymous ancestor, Jacob (Israel), is especially characterized as one who "stayed in tents" (Gen 25:27). Furthermore, in the book of Exodus, God himself instituted the Tent of Meeting. Genesis is not anti-technology.

However, it quickly becomes clear that Genesis was aware of both the potentials and dangers of technology as the otherwise positive portrayal of these technological advances (Gen 4:17–22) is darkened by the immediate subsequent narration of Lamech's murderous boasting (Gen 4:23–24). Lamech, the father of those who advanced ancient technology, boasts about killing a "youth" for "bruising him" (Gen 4:23). As Blenkinsopp has noted, "At this point technological achievement becomes suspect."[65] The positive contributions to humanity made by these technological innovators do not prevent the spread of violence and wickedness. Genesis here warns of technology separated from morality.[66]

Modern implications. Following two world wars in the first half of the twentieth century, the myth of progress has been tempered considerably from the Enlightenment optimism that previously dominated the philosophical mindset of the West. However, progress continues to be an underlying current in contemporary

---

63. Westermann, *Genesis 1–11*, 343, notes that at this point Genesis views technological development as "a function of the blessing God bestows on his creatures to enable the creatures themselves to make basic discoveries."
64. E.g., Gabriel, "Kainitengenealogie."
65. Blenkinsopp, *Creation*, 87.
66. Ibid., 90.

thought. This is especially so in the area of technological progress. In the mind of many, the great advances in technology surely hold the potential for the improvement of life. In fact, the perceived salvific potential of science and technology continues to hold a position in the West that used to be reserved for God in the pre-critical era.[67] The ancient warnings in Genesis about technology divorced from morality seem very relevant even now in the twenty-first century.[68]

The Rise of Religion
Returning to the text of Genesis 4, immediately following this genealogical aside concerned with the violence of Lamech, people are said to "invoke the name of the Lord" for the first time (4:26). To invoke a deity means "to offer worship by external acts."[69] Therefore, this text may be referring to the origins of religious practice.[70] This notice of the beginnings of organized worship separated from the origins of technology is interesting in light of contemporary ancient Near Eastern literature. In ancient Phoenician texts, beginnings of both technologies and worship are mentioned together as part of the account of origins.[71] However, Genesis contrasts the two and clearly asserts that advanced

---

67. Even in the postwar period, optimism showed itself in predictions that the workweek would be shorter due to technological advances. In the 1950s there were predictions that in the 1990s people would have "a twenty-two hour week, a six month workyear, or a standard retirement age of thirty-eight." See, Schor, *Overworked American*, 4. Similarly, in Canada it was predicted that the workweek would be shortened significantly (which has obviously not happened). Cf. LaPlante, "Leisure in Canada by 1980," 31.

68. On the other hand, Westermann, *Genesis 1–11*, 343–44, points out that a balance is necessary between religion and technology. He writes, "The question arises then whether the one-sided attitude of western theology in favor of intellectual pursuits and the ever-increasing alienation of theology from the natural sciences, technology, and the social sciences represents a false development that has contributed to the decline of the significance of theology today." Though Genesis warns of technology devoid of religion, religion devoid of the reality of creation (as seen in the sciences etc.) is also lamentable and against God's original ideal.

69. Blenkinsopp, *Creation*, 89.
70. Ibid., 89.
71. Attridge and Oden, *Philo of Byblos*, 42–43.

technology (the seven innovators of Gen 4:17–22) does not lead to an enlightened civilization (e.g., Lamech's murderous boasting). What is needed is religion—invoking the name of Yahweh (Gen 4:26). Genesis 1–11 is indeed skeptical about the idea of progress exclusive of religion. This suggests that the reason why the author included with his genealogy this aside regarding Lamech was to undermine the idea of progress. Technology cannot improve humans—only God can do that. Genesis purposefully sets the beginning of religion over against the development of technology.

Empire Building: Technology and False Religion Unite
The danger of technological advance divorced from true religion comes to the fore in the story of the builders of Babel in Genesis 11. As we have seen throughout Genesis 1–11, the critique of polytheistic culture was implicit, and is more clearly seen when read in comparison with ancient Near Eastern texts. However, in Genesis 11, with the story of the city and the tower at Babel, the critique becomes explicit, as "Babel" is the Hebrew word for Babylon (everywhere else in the Old Testament where the word is used, it is translated "Babylon"). Thus, the critique explicitly targets a known contemporary culture rather than implicitly critiquing ancient Near Eastern theology and cosmology generally.

The story is very well known, but some of the important details are often overlooked or taken to be simply historical notices that are not very relevant to the interpretation of the story.[72] In order to understand the story, it is important to read it in the context of both its ancient Near Eastern environment and its immediate literary context in Genesis 1–11.

The City
First it is important to observe what is being built. Not just a tower, but "a city and a tower" (Gen 11:4). Though the tower

---

72. E.g., regarding the note on brick technology, Blenkinsopp *Creation*, 165, notes that this "looks like an explanation addressed to readers resident in Palestine where stone was plentiful and used for building."

became the main focus of later interpretations, both the city and the tower deserve our attention. First, the attempt to build a city evinces a movement towards urbanization, which was a technological advance from tent dwelling.[73] Urban centers featured more "cooperative living," which allowed "more people to live together in a defined region, as it would allow for large-scale irrigation and excess grain production."[74] In light of this, the potential benefits to human existence are readily apparent.

In the ancient world, stories about the founding of cities were an important part of people's traditions and heritage.[75] Furthermore, in ancient Near Eastern literature, stories about the founding of cities usually followed a fairly standard format and generally included three things:

> [1] a description of the natural resources which attracted the builder (water supply, grazing and crop land, natural defenses), [2] the special attributes of the builder (unusual strength and/or wisdom) and [3] the guidance of the patron god.[76]

Since these elements were standard in such stories, it is instructive to notice what details Genesis 11 provides in this regard.

1. Reasons for Choosing the Site
The reasons for the choosing of this particular site are not elaborated in any detail in Genesis 11. We are told that they simply found a valley in the land of Shinar and settled there (Gen 11:2).

2. Attributes of the Builders
We are told two important details regarding the characteristics of the builders of Babel: (a) they all had one language; and (b) they were technological innovators.

a. One language: The reference to the monolingual environment is significant given the present literary context of Genesis 11. Already the previous chapter (the so-called "Table of Nations") refers to different languages spoken by various people

---

73. Walton and Matthews, *Bible Background*, 41.
74. Ibid., 41.
75. Ibid., 34. E.g., founding of Rome by Romulus and Remus.
76. Ibid.

groups who settle in their own territories (Gen 10:5, 20, 31).[77] Thus, the builders of Babel are presented as resisting both "linguistic differentiation" and the spread of humanity into different groups and territories.[78] Blenkinsopp suggests that the builders of Babel were aware that language is an "instrument of power, control and coercion."[79] Their resistance to the way the world was developing shows some advanced thinking and the knowledge that maintaining linguistic identity may aid in preventing loss of identity and strengthen the unity and security of the group.

b. Technological innovators: The builders of Babel are also presented as creative visionaries who pioneer the use of kiln dried bricks in monumental architecture instead of stone.

> And they said to one another, "Come, let us make bricks, and burn them thoroughly." And they had brick for stone, and bitumen for mortar (Gen 11:3).

---

77. Of course some suggest that the story of Babel moves "back in time" since different languages were already referenced in Genesis 10. E.g., Walton, *Genesis*, 371. However, this is not clear from the literary context but is an assumption made due to modern concerns with chronology. There is no sign from the text that a backward temporal transition occurs, contra 2 Kings 20, which clearly occurs out of chronological order with the story of the Assyrian invasion of Hezekiah's Judah. In this instance of purposeful chronological displacement the author signals this by noting God's promise to "deliver you and this city out of the hand of the king of Assyria; I will defend this city for my own sake and for my servant David's sake" (2 Kgs 20:6), which clearly antedates the events of 2 Kings 18–19 and even quotes verbatim from 2 Kgs 19:34 ("For I will defend this city to save it, for my own sake and for the sake of my servant David."). Furthermore, the intent of the text may not be to suggest that "all the earth" in Gen 11:1 means the "entire planet" or "entire population" as a modern reader may understand the phrase. As Walton, *Genesis*, 371–72, writes, "The mention of 'all the earth' . . . gives the modern reader a universal feel to the passage, but that sense may be somewhat mitigated when we recall that the Hebrew word translated 'earth' also often means 'land' and is more narrowly defined. We cannot afford to jump to unwarranted conclusions about the universality of the references."

78. Blenkinsopp, *Creation*, 168.

79. Ibid., 168.

In ancient Israel stone was readily available; however, in Mesopotamia this was not the case. This new technology allowed for the building of monumental architecture in Mesopotamia without having to quarry stone from far away and transport it to the site.[80] In light of the fact that the special attributes of city founders are invariably highlighted in ancient accounts of city building, the portrayal of the builders of Babylon as technological innovators is likely a significant element in the story. Of course a focus on technological innovation should not be too surprising given the critique of innovative technology found in Genesis 4 (see above).

3. Divine Patronage

As mentioned above, ancient Near Eastern accounts of city building invariably refer to the guidance of the patron god in the founding of the city. However, in Genesis 11 no such role is given to the deity. In fact, far from being involved in the project, God must "come down" (Gen 11:5) to see the tower that humans are building.[81] In other words, this project is pure human ambition representing the best (technological innovation) and the worst (the establishment of a self-serving pagan religion) of humanity.

The Tower

Key to understanding the sin of Babel is understanding what the text means by the "tower." Unfortunately, the reference to the tower with its "head in the heavens" (11:4) has frequently been misunderstood. It has been popularly thought that the builders of Babel were attempting to build a tower so high that they would reach "heaven." However, the ancients were not so obtuse as to think they could actually reach the top of the sky with a human-

---

80. This technology developed near the close of the fourth millennium BC and was quite effective. As Walton writes, "the resulting product, using bitumen as a mastic, proved waterproof and as sturdy as stone. Since it was an expensive process, it was used only for important public buildings" (Walton and Matthews, *Bible Background*, 41).

81. Which is humorous in light of their goal to make a tower with its "head in the heavens" (Gen 11:4).

made building. What is in view here is a ziggurat. This is clear from the description "head in the heavens" (Gen 11:4) which is found in Mesopotamian writings and used almost exclusively for ziggurats.[82]

A ziggurat may look something like a pyramid but is nothing of the sort. It is filled entirely with dirt and has no burial chamber or passages of any kind inside. It did not even function as a temple (though a temple was usually adjacent to it and used for worship). Its main function was to carry a stairway that led to the top of the ziggurat. On the top of the stairway was a shrine to a god or gods. It was a hotel room of sorts for a god who was on a journey down to earth. The stairway represented a bridge between the realm of the gods and earth. At the top of the ziggurat the god could be refreshed with rest and food (which the priests would replenish regularly) and then come down the stairway to bless the people. The ziggurat functioned to provide for the needs of the god in order that the god would be obligated to return the favor and bless the people. In other words, the ziggurat was a mechanism for manipulating the deity.[83]

In light of the builders' resistance to the world as it had unfolded in Genesis 10 (resisting linguistic differentiation and resisting the spread of humanity), the project of the city and a tower represent the concentration of political power. Cutting edge technology made their impressive project possible and the creation of a potent religious symbol legitimated it. Because their project functioned as a means to manipulate the deity, the builders could be assured of divine support. The tyrannical twosome of self-sufficient technology and self-serving religion represents a human bid for self-achieved security. Herein lie the origins of Empire-building.

Considering the technological progress and oppressive religion that harnesses the power of the divine, one can understand God's statement that "this is only the beginning of what they will

---

82. E.g., the description of a ziggurat by Warad-Sin, King of Larsa, states, "He made it as high as a mountain and made its head touch heaven" (Frayne, *Royal Inscriptions*, 208).

83. Walton, *Genesis*, 383.

do; nothing that they propose to do will now be impossible for them" (11:6). The twentieth century has shown what humans are capable of when armed with a combination of technological advancement and ideological propaganda. God's statements concerning human potential ring true in light of the wars, ethnic cleansing, genocide, nuclear and biological weaponry, and ecological degradation that flourished in the previous century and continue to the present.[84] In light of this reality, Genesis 1–11 can be read as an admonition concerning the dangers and ambiguities of inexhaustible technological "progress," especially when coupled with a powerful and persuasive ideology.[85]

It is important to remember that in its day, Babylon was regarded as the religious, intellectual, and cultural capital of the world. It was the showpiece of civilization, synonymous with high culture and advanced technology. This makes the explicit criticism (i.e., Genesis names Babylon outright) all the more audacious. The name Babylon meant "gate of God." However, Genesis confronts this potent ideology and undermines its foundations. According to Gen 11:9 Babel means "confusion" or "folly" (*balal* in Hebrew). While Babylon's ambition and technology impressed the ancient world, God needed to "come down" (11:5) in order to see this tower that supposedly reached the divine realm.

Modern Implications

While our technologies are clearly more advanced than those of Babylon, is our wisdom any greater? Are we more conscious of our limitations or more aware of our capacity for immorality than they?[86] In 1992, Neil Postman suggested that the United States of America had become a technopoly, that is, a culture in which "all forms of cultural life" submit to "the sovereignty of technique and technology."[87] For many, the authority of science

---

84. Blenkinsopp, *Creation*, 170.
85. Ibid.
86. Ibid.
87. Postman, *Technopoly*, 52.

and technology has replaced belief in the authority of God or religion. According to Postman, a characteristic feature of a technopoly is the systemic lack of a "transcendent sense of purpose or meaning."[88] We can see this in many ways with the internet, which provides plenty of information, but not wisdom. Social media imparts hundreds of "friends," but few real friends. According to Postman, too much information leads to information becoming "essentially meaningless."[89] Scientific truth, though so powerful and enabling in many ways, fails in discerning the truth regarding the fundamental questions about life. Who are we? What is our purpose? How should we live? Genesis 1–11 sets out to point to where those answers might be found.

In the end, the goal of the entire narrative of Genesis 1–11 is to be found in God's calling of Abraham and the covenant God makes with him.[90] Though God created the world "good," the spread of evil corrupted it. Humans repeatedly attempt to make a name for themselves and to grasp at the divine through their misguided attempts at self-sufficiency.[91] In Genesis 1–11, "things go wrong when humans take the initiatives; humankind tends to destroy what God has made good."[92] However, there is an observable pattern in Genesis 1–11 of the "spread of sin"

---

88. Ibid., 63.

89. Ibid., 77.

90. As Walton, *Genesis*, 382, suggests, "the purpose of Genesis 1–11 was to show the need for the covenant." Similarly, Clines, *Theme of the Pentateuch*, 86, concludes that "To link the primaeval history with the patriarchal narrative specifies the thrust of the primaeval history . . . [it] is the prelude to the promises and their fulfilment."

91. Throughout the narrative, there has been a striving by humans to be like God. In the Garden, the forbidden fruit was considered desirable because it would make one like God (Gen 3:5–6). In Genesis 6, we see what Wenham has called "grasping at immortality" with the intermarriage between the sons of God and the daughters of men (Wenham, *Genesis 1–15*, 146). The Nephilim, mentioned in this passage, are said to be "men of the name" (Gen 6:4). Again, in the story of Babel, the builders sought to make a name for themselves (Gen 11:4).

92. Clines, *Theme of the Pentateuch*, 86.

followed by the "spread of grace."[93] As humans sin, God responds with punishment, but also with grace. As Clines writes:

> God not only punishes Adam and Eve, but also withholds the threatened penalty of death; he not only drives out Cain, but also puts his mark of protection upon him; not only sends the Flood, but saves the human race alive in preserving Noah and his family.[94]

Despite the spread of evil in creation, God responds by continually mitigating the consequences and seeking out ways to bless his creation in spite of itself. Significantly, in the story of Babel, there is a punishment, but no corresponding 'grace' element until the calling of Abraham at the beginning of the next chapter (Gen 12). Finally God sets out to make Abraham's "name great" and thereby bless "all the families of the earth" (Gen 12:3).

Conclusion

Though sometimes entertaining, Genesis 1–11 was not simply written to entertain. Though concerned with ancient history, these chapters were not primarily written to provide historical details. For the biblical authors, the Genesis stories were a vehicle for expressing truths about life—both corporate and individual life—and to reveal the truth about God.[95] Genesis addresses matters relevant for individuals in both ancient and modern societies and reflects on the human condition, challenging our modern self-understanding. Though no clear answer is given regarding the origins of evil, humans are presented as beings capable of choosing their own course of action, and are not inhibited from doing so by their Creator.[96] Furthermore, Genesis presents a God keenly interested in his creation, despite its faults.

This gracious and loving concern with his creation leads to God initiating a covenant with Abraham, which culminates in the

93. Ibid., 70.
94. Ibid.
95. Blenkinsopp, *Creation*, 16.
96. Ibid., 10.

work of God's Son who invites us into a transformative relationship with him that will impact our way of being in the world. Rather than making a name for ourselves, we must trust in the name that God has made great (Phil 2:9)—that of his Son, Jesus. For it is written, "Salvation is found in no one else, for there is no other name under heaven given to humans by which we must be saved" (Acts 4:12).

Bibliography

Alexander, T. D. *From Paradise to the Promised Land: An Introduction to the Pentateuch.* Grand Rapids: Baker Academic, 2002.

Arnold, Bill T., and Bryan Beyer. *Readings from the Ancient Near East: Primary Sources for Old Testament Study.* Encountering Biblical Studies. Grand Rapids: Baker Academic, 2002.

Attridge, Harold W., and Robert A. Oden. *Philo of Byblos: The Phoenician History.* CBQMS. Washington: Catholic Biblical Association of America, 1981.

Bird, Phyllis A. "'Male and Female He Created Them': Genesis 1:27b in the Context of the Priestly Account of Creation." In *I Studied Inscriptions before the Flood*, edited by Richard S. Hess and David Toshio Tsumura, 329–61. Winona Lake: Eisenbrauns, 1994.

Blenkinsopp, Joseph. *Creation, Un-Creation, Re-Creation: A Discursive Commentary on Genesis 1–11.* London: T. & T. Clark, 2011.

———. *The Pentateuch: An Introduction to the First Five Books of the Bible.* Anchor Bible Reference Library. New York: Doubleday, 1992.

Brown, Francis, S. R. Driver, and Charles A. Briggs. *Hebrew and English Lexicon of the Old Testament.* Oxford: Clarendon, 1907.

Clines, David J. A. *The Theme of the Pentateuch.* JSOTSup 10. 2nd ed. Sheffield: Sheffield Academic, 1997.

Dalley, Stephanie. *Myths from Mesopotamia.* New York: Oxford University Press, 1991.

Foster, Benjamin R. "Atra-Hasis." In *The Context of Scripture: Canonical Compositions from the Biblical World.* Vol. 1: 450–53. Leiden: Brill, 1997.

———. "Epic of Creation." In *The Context of Scripture: Canonical Compositions from the Biblical World.* Vol. 1: 390–402. Leiden: Brill, 1997.

Frayne, Douglas. *Royal Inscriptions of Mesopotamia: Old Babylonian Period (2003–1595 BC).* Toronto: University of Toronto Press, 1990.

Fretheim, Terence E. *Creation Untamed: The Bible, God, and Natural Disasters.* Theological Explorations for the Church Catholic. Grand Rapids: Baker Academic, 2010.

Gabriel, Johannes. "Die Kainitengenealogie: Gn 4,17–24." *Biblica* 40 (1959) 409–27.

Gunkel, Hermann. *Schöpfung und Chaos in Urzeit und Endzeit: Eine religionsgeschichtliche Untersuchung über Gen 1 und Ap Joh 12.* Göttingen: Vandenhoeck & Ruprecht, 1895.

Hasel, Gerhard F. "Polemic Nature of the Genesis Cosmology." *EvQ* 46 (1974) 81–102.

Heidel, Alexander. *The Babylonian Genesis: The Story of Creation.* Chicago: University of Chicago Press, 1951.

Kapelrud, Arvid S. "Mythological Features in Genesis Chapter 1 and the Author's Intentions." *VT* 24 (1974) 178–86.

Lambert, Wilfred G. "A New Look at the Babylonian Background of Genesis." In *I Studied Inscriptions before the Flood*, edited by Richard S. Hess and David Toshio Tsumura, 96–113. Winona Lake: Eisenbrauns, 1994.

LaPlante, Marc. "Leisure in Canada by 1980." In *Leisure in Canada: The Proceedings of the Montmorency Conference on Leisure, 2–6 September 1969*. Ottawa: Fitness and Amateur Sport Directorate, Department of National Health and Welfare, 1969.

Moltmann, Jürgen. *God in Creation: A New Theology of Creation and the Spirit of God*. Gifford Lectures. Minneapolis: Fortress, 1991.

Postman, Neil. *Technopoly: The Surrender of Culture to Technology*. New York: Knopf, 1992.

Schor, Juliet. *The Overworked American: The Unexpected Decline of Leisure*. New York: Basic Books, 1991.

Taylor, J. Glen. *Yahweh and the Sun: Biblical and Archaeological Evidence for Sun Worship in Ancient Israel*. JSOTSup 111. Sheffield: JSOT Press, 1993.

Tsumura, David Toshio. *The Earth and the Waters in Genesis 1 and 2: A Linguistic Investigation*. JSOTSup 83. Sheffield: Sheffield Academic, 1989.

———. "Genesis and Ancient Near Eastern Stories of Creation and Flood: An Introduction." In *I Studied Inscriptions before the Flood*, edited by Richard S. Hess and David Toshio Tsumura, 27–57. Winona Lake: Eisenbrauns, 1994.

Walton, John H. *Genesis*. NIVAC. Grand Rapids: Zondervan, 2001.

Walton, John H., and Victor Harold Matthews. *The IVP Bible Background Commentary: Genesis-Deuteronomy*. Downers Grove; IL: InterVarsity, 1997.

Watson, Francis. *Text, Church and World: Biblical Interpretation in Theological Perspective*. Edinburgh: T. & T. Clark, 1994.

Watts, Rikki E. "Making Sense of Genesis 1." *Stimulus* 12 no. 4 (2004) 2–12.

Wenham, Gordon J. *Genesis 1–15*. WBC. Waco: Word, 1991.

Westermann, Claus. *Genesis 1–11: A Commentary*. Minneapolis: Augsburg, 1984.

WHOSE PSYCHOLOGY? WHICH CHRISTIANITY?*

Russell D. Kosits
Redeemer University College, Ancaster, ON

The publication of *Psychology & Christianity: Five Views*, (ed. Eric L. Johnson. IVP, 2010), marks a significant occasion in the ongoing faith-learning dialogue in psychology. The first edition of the book, *Psychology & Christianity: Four Views* (ed. Eric L. Johnson and Stanton L. Jones. IVP, 2000) has had a powerful effect in shaping this dialogue. From 2008 through 2010 alone, for example, there were approximately 29 new adoptions of the book for university-level courses (this represents about 25 percent of the CCCU[1] member institutions). Since the first edition appeared in 2000, the number of university course adoptions has likely far exceeded that number. "Perhaps the best evidence for the influence of the first edition," one former staff member at IVP said, "is the publication of the second. In a sense the first

---

* I have incurred many debts since I submitted this article for publication in February 2011. Thanks to Lois Dow for her willingness to accept several unsolicited revisions and additions to the original article, to my anonymous reviewer, to my colleagues in the Social Sciences Division here at Redeemer (who read a version of the manuscript during my tenure review), particularly David Koyzis, Laura Lunchies, and Jim Vanderwoerd (who carefully read all or portions of the final version and provided thoughtful feedback), to my friend Bruce Johnson who gave the first manuscript an exacting edit, and to my student Christina Garchinski who shared her artistic talents to enhance and beautify the figures. Though none of these would agree with everything I say here, this essay has been improved because of their efforts.

1. The member institutions of the CCCU (Council of Christian Colleges and Universities) are committed to pursuing higher education in an intentionally "Christ-centered" fashion, where faith and learning are "integrated" in meaningful ways.

edition got the ball rolling on a lot of questions and influenced the terms of discussion enough that a new edition was needed."[2]

This certainly fits my experience. Over the last eight years I have been a faculty member at two Christian universities, and have used *Psychology & Christianity* as a textbook for six of those years. Three of the four views presented in the first edition have had a profound impact on my thinking and teaching. As the book has appeared in a new edition, it seems an appropriate time to solidify past gains and to begin the process of dialoguing with the new text. To this end, I aim to do several things in this paper. First, I describe a theological and philosophical framework for thinking about the relationship between psychology and Christianity—a still-developing framework initially conceived in my interactions with the first edition of the book. In light of this framework, I then provide something of an in-depth retrospective review of the first edition, introducing the categories of "modern perspectivalism," and "postmodern perspectivalism." Next, I offer a third—Reformed and Reformational[3]—perspectivalism, a position that attempts to synthesize the key insights of the viewpoints expressed in the first edition. After evaluating the second edition of the textbook in light of this position, I conclude with some thoughts on the question of Christian engagement with the still-modern culture of contemporary academic psychology.

---

2. My thanks to Heather Mascarello, print publicity manager at IVP, for providing the data, and Emily Varner, former academic sales manager at IVP, for the quote.

3. By "Reformed" I have in mind a variety of Christian experience characterized by a vital commitment to the truths summarized in the Reformed confessions of the sixteenth and seventeenth centuries. By "Reformational" I refer to the attempt to philosophize within the bounds of this confessional commitment, as exemplified by Dooyeweerd, Vollenhoven, and Clouser.

A Theological and Philosophical Framework for Conceptualizing the Relationship between Psychology and Christianity

As historians such as Norman Fiering[4] have shown, the question of the relation of "pagan" learning to Christianity is an ancient one. Though the question easily predates the European settlement in North America (as Tertullian's famous ponderings regarding the relation of "Jerusalem and Athens" attest), it was a central concern in North America's oldest colleges. For example, in seventeenth-century Harvard and eighteenth-century Yale, students read William Ames's *Marrow of Theology*, which contained not only a systematic description of biblical teaching, but also aspects of a full-fledged theory of the relationship between theology and the liberal arts.[5] In subsequent generations, positions on the faith-learning question changed, yet Christian dominance of the North American university continued (in one form or another) for about three centuries. Though the subtle process of secularization had been underway since the mid-eighteenth century,[6] it was not until the early- to mid-twentieth century that universities began explicitly cutting their ties to their Christian roots. McMaster University, for example, whose motto remains, "All Things Cohere in Christ," did not officially break its ties to its Baptist roots until 1957.[7] So, the old question that is addressed in *Psychology & Christianity* takes on a new hue. For the first time in centuries, Christians would need to ask their questions about the relation of Jerusalem and Athens from *outside* the academies that they had established (none of the authors in the first edition, and only one of the authors in the second edition writes from a secular university).[8] Inevitably, then, the

---

4. Fiering, *Moral Philosophy*, 11–22.
5. Ames, *Marrow of Theology*; Miller, *New England Mind*, 154–80. For an exposition of the full-fledged theory, see Ames, *Technometry*.
6. Marsden, *Soul of the American University*.
7. Johnston, *McMaster University*, 261.
8. It is of course true that many Christians still teach and research within these now "secular" universities. But they most typically do so by asking *other* questions.

question must be reframed—how shall we relate "secular" learning to Christianity in a post-Christian era?

Which Christianity?
One question we must certainly address in this post-Christian context is, "Which Christianity do we desire to relate to secular learning?" The unwillingness to ask this question was—ironically enough—one of the major causes of secularization in the first place. As George Marsden has argued, as far back as the mid-eighteenth century, American educators dealt with the problem of Protestant pluralism by employing a "nonsectarian" strategy, which diminished theological distinctiveness and emphasized instead common moral convictions derived through a supposedly neutral and scientific methodology.[9] This discomfort with theological particularity eventuated in an academic environment where liberal Christian open-mindedness became the context of its own eventual abolition.

It would be unfair to characterize participants in the psychology-Christianity debate as moralistic or simply "nonsectarian"; we do nevertheless find a tendency—by no means universal—to advocate a "mere Christianity" approach. To put the matter differently, the issue might be framed as the dialectic between Erasmian and Lutheran sensibilities. The great humanist Erasmus desired to go *ad fontes* for the sake of personal change, with impatience toward and suspicion of theology as hair-splitting "scholastic" argumentation. Luther, of course, wanted to go back to Scripture in order to arrange the teachings of Scripture in a systematic and theological fashion.[10] In some ways Erasmus was right—it is more important to live well than to have every jot and tittle of one's theology straight. Yet in other ways, Luther was right—that unless we get our theology straight we will not be able to live well. Certainly, we will not be able to *theorize* as well as we might as Christians if we are not able or

---

9. Marsden, *Soul of the American University*.
10. For a discussion of Erasmus, see George, *Theology of the Reformers*, 46–49; González, *Story of Christianity*, 2:10–13; McGrath, *Reformation Thought*, 53–58.

willing to define our belief system. We should not, therefore, shy away from making theological assertions, particularly when we desire to articulate a position on the relationship between Christianity and psychology. Perhaps Luther overstated the case in his famous debate with Erasmus, "take away assertions, and you take away Christianity."[11] But Luther was right that when it comes to academic discussions such as his debate with Erasmus on free will or our discussion of the relation between Christianity and psychology: take away [theological][12] assertions and one soon begins to wonder just what we are trying to relate to psychology.

There are irenic, polemic, and interpersonal reasons for foregrounding theological assertions in any discussion of the relationship between psychology and Christianity. On the irenic side, Christianity is bigger than any one theological perspective. As Vern Poythress and John Frame have long argued, Scripture is a treasure trove that can be profitably studied from a multitude of perspectives.[13] Certainly this argument would apply to some extent to theological traditions, each of which may have a unique perspective that opens up the truth of Scripture. The extent to which a particular tradition offers unique and reliable insight into the Scripture is quite likely the extent to which a particular tradition would have something unique to contribute to psychology.

On a more polemic note, being explicit about one's theological convictions should make more evident the adequacy of such formulations. It is possible, after all, that some theological perspectives will more effectively frame the issues in question. Some theological perspectives will be more hermeneutically useful in engaging the world of secular psychology.

Interpersonally, explicitness about theological positions would also most likely be helpful in understanding why people

---

11. Rupp and Watson, eds., *Luther and Erasmus*, 106.

12. In this paper I define a theological assertion as one that attempts to coherently set forth biblical teaching on a particular topic, not necessarily one that comes from the academic discipline of theology.

13. Frame, *Doctrine of the Knowledge of God*, e.g., 191–94; Poythress, *Symphonic Theology*.

differ in their positions on the relation of psychology and Christianity in the first place. It is hard to have a discussion about the relation of psychology and Christianity when one's interlocutor has not told you what they mean by "Christianity."[14]

Given that one's position on the relationship between psychology and Christianity will inevitably reflect one's own (spoken or unspoken) theological commitments, it is only reasonable to expect me to outline the assumptions and influences I bring to the discussion. I belong to the Augustinian-Calvinist theological stream running through the Westminster Standards, Old Princeton Seminary in the nineteenth century, Westminster Seminary in the twentieth, now represented by institutions such as Reformed Theological Seminary (main campus Orlando, FL). My main theological and philosophical influences include Augustine, Calvin, the Westminster Standards, Jonathan Edwards, Abraham Kuyper, Herman Dooyeweerd, Dirk Vollenhoven, Cornelius Van Til, Roy Clouser, Michael Horton, and John Frame. In what follows I will outline briefly some aspects of this perspective that are crucial for relating psychology and Christianity.[15]

God's Sovereignty, the Two Books of God's Self-revelation, and the Glory of God: The sovereignty of God is a crucial insight for theoretical work in psychology. As Cornelius Van Til maintained decades ago, the fact that God is in control of "whatsoever comes to pass" is a truth that ensures that all things are *meaningful* because they have been pre-interpreted by God, and that all science is therefore *hermeneutical* in the sense that we cannot ultimately understand what we study until we have some (limited, creaturely) insight into this pre-interpretation.

---

14. In other words, explicitness about theological commitments can facilitate honest *dialogue*. See Johnson, "Gaining Understanding," 299–301 for a helpful discussion of the importance of dialogue.

15. To use the language of Johnson, what follows is something of an initial sketch of a Reformed and Reformational "metasystem" that holds together ideas that at first may seem contradictory. See ibid., 304–10.

Scripture (which tells us about the sovereignty of God)[16] affords insight into this pre-interpretation. Though the Bible tends[17] not to provide the data of psychology, it provides the ultimate framework for the interpretation of the data of psychology, apart from which psychological science suffers greatly (as will be elaborated below). This framework may be helpfully summarized by—though not reduced to or replaced by—the traditional scheme of "creation, fall, and redemption."

The traditional idea that God has revealed himself in "two books" is crucial. Scripture and creation both *richly* reveal God.[18] The fact that God not only created all things, but also providentially sustains all things, ensures that the "two books" cohere, and both must be consulted if one desires to understand the world in which we live. The fatal mistake in any discussion of the relation of psychology and Christianity is *source asymmetry*—i.e., inappropriately emphasizing one book over the other. The idea here isn't that there should always be "equal parts Bible and science" in psychology. Instead, the real challenge is to learn to read both books together, giving to each its own authority, necessity, sufficiency, and perspicuity.[19]

Any understanding of the pre-interpretation afforded by the Word of God must include the glory of God. The goal of both

---

16. For an excellent biblical defense of the traditional Calvinist doctrine of God's absolute sovereignty, see Frame, *Doctrine of God*, ch. 4.

17. In my own Kuyperian tradition of relating faith and learning, some seem to insist that Scripture *never* provides data for any special science (like psychology). To pre-judge Scripture in this way is unscriptural. A Christian scholar always needs in every aspect of life to ask, "What does the Bible say?" and should not decide beforehand that the Bible has nothing to say about a particular topic. Still, for the most part, the multitudinous data of any science (including psychology) tend to be found outside of the Scriptures.

18. In other words, Scripture and creation are not *thin* revelations of God, but are rather *crammed* with God. See Powlison, "Do You See?"

19. This is the way Cornelius Van Til formulated the matter. Just as the Westminster Confession speaks of the necessity, authority, sufficiency, and perspicuity of Scripture, we ought also to speak of the same characteristics of the other "book" of God's revelation.

texts is the same—the glory and praise of the Triune God.[20] If we stop at mere description, explanation, prediction, or control[21] and do not end in doxology[22] we have not fully exegeted either "text."[23]

I would therefore maintain that the traditional Reformed emphasis on the glory of God must also be an emphasis of any effort to relate psychology and Christianity. God's main purpose in all that he does is his own glory. The chief end of psychology too is to glorify God. It follows that, if God always remains simply a hidden or underlying assumption of our psychological work, we have not fully discharged our responsibilities.

This set of considerations therefore raises a set of questions to be asked of any attempt to relate psychology and Christianity: is the sovereign, self-revealing, and self-glorifying God at the center of the approach? Are both books of God's self-revelation given their due?

The "Kuyperian Paradox": A great challenge of Christian scholarship is walking the razor's edge between accommodation (uncritically accepting the assertions and assumptions of "secular" science) and world-flight (uncritically rejecting the productions of "secular" science). This is what I would call "the Kuyperian[24] paradox," that two, seemingly mutually exclusive

---

20. The classic defense of the idea that God's main purpose in making the world was his own glory is Jonathan Edwards's "Dissertation" on "the End for which God Created the World," in Edwards, "Two Dissertations."

21. These are the four traditional goals of psychological research. See Goodwin, *Research in Psychology*, 25–26.

22. There are analogies here between the approach I am advocating and the ill-fated "doxological science" of my Presbyterian forebears, as told in Bozeman, *Protestants in an Age of Science*. There is an enormous difference, however, between the failed project of Baconian inductivism and the "engaged presuppositionalism" that I will advocate below.

23. Still, it should be kept in mind that creation not only praises God (Ps 19:1), but it also groans (Rom 8:22). Any explication of the creation's praise of God must recognize that in this "old order of things" (Rev 21:4) creation's praise is always intermingled with lament.

24. Named, of course, after the great Dutch thinker, Abraham Kuyper, who had a keen sense of antithesis, and yet was also a champion of common grace.

principles must be embraced by a Christian scholar.[25] The first of these is the notion of "antithesis"; the second, the notion of "common grace."

Biblically, the idea of antithesis traces back to Gen 3:15, where God placed "enmity" between the seed of the woman and the seed of the serpent, and all of biblical history can be viewed with some profit through that lens.[26] Philosophically and theologically, Augustine gave the most famous expression to this idea, arguing that the drama of human history has to do with the conflict between the two cities, the *civitas terrena*, or earthly city characterized by love of self, and the *civitas Dei*, or city of God, characterized by the love of YHWH. In principle and at root, these two cities disagree fundamentally about the purpose and meaning of life and about the source of true human happiness and flourishing. Within science, these differences manifest themselves in a variety of ways, and usually *subtly*. Antithesis does not imply an overt, over-the-top, Dawkins-like animosity toward religion.

Rather, antithesis manifests itself epistemologically and hermeneutically. In the City of God, the world is (ideally, at least) understood for what it is, a revelation of God, and the Scripture (as the Word of the God who is the light in which we see light—Ps 36:9) is given its primary epistemological place. Hermeneutically, careful and rigorous scientific and theoretical activity conducted properly in the light of Scripture ought to lead to the praise and glory of God. In the *civitas terrena*, any reference to Scripture as authoritative in the realm of science is ruled out.

This is not to say that Bible study ought to replace careful scientific work—far from it. This isn't to say that the Bible is "a

---

My main disagreement with Kuyper, however, would be in the realm of apologetics. Because of the antithesis, Kuyper thought (evidential) apologetics futile. Though I don't disagree with him on the problems with evidential apologetics, I do think that twentieth-century developments in apologetics raise some interesting possibilities. My own position will be described below.

25. Hence, a definition of paradox that I would embrace is, "a statement that seems contradictory, unbelievable, or absurd but that may actually be true in fact" (*Webster's New Universal Unabridged Dictionary*, 1983).

26. Currid, *Study Commentary on Genesis*, 131.

scientific textbook." But it is to say that without the Scriptures, scientific work will not flourish as it ought to. In particular, without the Scriptures, science inevitably suffers *hermeneutically*. In the city of man, the world is misinterpreted in multitudinous ways, but all such misinterpretations share this fundamental (and typically unspoken) assumption: *if* God exists, he is not relevant to scientific activity. And whenever science is carried out *autonomously* (without reference to God and his Word), it inevitably misses the theological point of its work.

It is important to note that many thinkers in this tradition have emphasized that the antithesis runs deeply through the Christian heart as well. Part of the "old man" in Adam desires to maintain autonomy, to engage in scientific and theoretical activity without any reference to God and outside of scriptural revelation. Indeed, from the very earliest days of the church, semi-autonomous reason (reason that has its own competence in its own sphere) has been embraced by substantial portions of the church.[27] Nevertheless, and as I will argue, such autonomy is ultimately, as Van Til often put it, "self-frustrative" and undermines not only the claims of the gospel but also the goals of science itself.

It is equally important to affirm the seemingly-contrary reality of common grace. Just as the antithesis runs through every citizen of the *civitas Dei*, it is likewise the case that God restrains sin within the *civitas terrena* and lavishes many good gifts upon its citizens, resulting in scientific and theoretical activity of the highest quality (oftentimes far exceeding the quality of work in the humble *civitas Dei*). A Christian scholar is therefore obligated to embrace these good gifts of God.[28] The affirmation of common grace should emphasize the goodness of creation and the joy and wholesomeness of scientific discovery *per se*. It should also emphasize, indeed, the brilliant scientific work that is being conducted *right now*.

This, then, is the second series of questions that must be asked of any approach attempting to relate mainstream psychological science and Christianity: does this approach attempt to

---

27. Clouser, *Myth of Religious Neutrality*, 98–99.
28. This famous argument is found in Calvin, *Institutes*, II.II.12–17.

walk the razor's edge, affirming both common grace and antithesis, or is one or the other emphasized?

The Modes of God's Providential Control: In the "Reformational" philosophical tradition of Herman Dooyeweerd, Dirk Vollenhoven, Roy Clouser, and others, the assumption of the sustaining and directing providence of God—alongside our pretheoretical intuitions of the lawfulness and normativity of the world—is elaborated so as to articulate a notion of "modalities," or "aspects," which have to do with the characteristic and irreducible ways that God's creatures function in this world. When articulated within the traditional categories of the Reformed confessions, the idea may be expressed thus—one of the ways that God providentially controls the entirety of his creation is through the regularity of "laws" and "norms." These modes of providential control would include, for example, mathematical and biological laws (which are inviolable), and aesthetic and economic norms (which are violable, but only at a cost). It is this lawful control of the universe that makes proximate-level science (i.e., the reading of the book of God's works in such a way as to elaborate the lawfulness and normativity of creation—i.e., the *what* and the *how*) possible. The book of God's Words, on the other hand, generally provides for ultimate-level interpretation. It, generally speaking, answers the *why* questions.

This philosophical elaboration of the notion of the sovereignty of God is useful in three main ways. First, it helps us to understand common grace. The Spirit of God can restrain sin directly, of course. But all creatures are also subject to the laws and norms that govern creaturely life. Proximate-level success in life (including scientific and theoretical life) requires "obedience" to these norms. Scientific work violating the norms of logic,[29] for example, will most likely never be published. Likewise, scientific manuscripts that violate aesthetic norms (such as clarity of expression) will most likely suffer the same fate. Certainly these examples illustrate that norms are applied differently

---

29. We will leave aside the complexities involved in the articulation of these laws.

through history and in different cultures. Nevertheless, we all live and move and have our being in God's world, and we are all alike constrained by its lawful and normed given-ness.

The notion of modality is also useful in that it helps us to understand the typical scholarly moves within the *civitas terrena*. Theoretical life, like all of life, is ultimately religious—there must inevitably be some ultimate and irreducible criterion by which we make sense of the world around us. As Reformational thinkers have long noted, scholars who do not give theoretical primacy to God will inevitably give primacy to some aspect of God's creation. Failing to worship God, we worship the creature. By forcing a mere aspect of God's creation to account for all reality, one asks too much of the creature. The typical result is "reductionism." Within psychology today, the *biotic* aspect tends to be accorded primacy—proximate-level findings are routinely and explicitly interpreted as being ultimately due to the products or by-products of unguided natural selection.[30] Though survival and reproduction are certainly key aspects of human functioning, the distortive nature of such explanations becomes evident, especially when theorists attempt to account for things like awe, language, or music (for example) in such reductive terms.[31] Part of our task in engaging the world of "secular" psychological science, then, is detecting these reductive moves.

The need then, it would seem, would be for non-reductive psychological theories, which brings us to the final benefit of such an approach. The notion of modality gives us a sense of the complexity of psychological functioning in humans, which is related not only to the biotic, but also to the linguistic, aesthetic, and ethical, for example. A full-orbed and non-reductive

---

30. We may also see this tendency even at the more proximate level of "entity" theories, but these connections are subtle and I do not think inevitable. For a discussion of entity theories, see Clouser, *Myth of Religious Neutrality*, 72–76.

31. For such a reductive account of awe, see Keltner, *Born to be Good*, ch. 12. For a reductive account of language, see Pinker, *Language Instinct*, ch. 11. A reductive account of music may be found in Levitin, *Your Brain on Music*, ch. 9.

approach will attempt to keep this complexity in view, using "a multidimensional explanatory methodology appropriate to the subject matter in hand."[32]

Thus, the third question I will ask of each approach is whether it attempts to elucidate the complex modal inter-relatedness of psychological functioning or tends toward reductionism.

Presuppositonal Apologetics: The reader may recall that Gen 3:15 is the foundational text teaching the principle of the antithesis. The "enmity" between the *civitas Dei* and the *civitas terrena* makes worldview conflict within science inevitable. Within the *civitas terrena*, science becomes one of the primary ways the knowledge of God revealed in creation is suppressed (Rom 1:18). Within the *civitas Dei,* science (properly understood) elaborates on Ps 19:1, showing in countless specific ways how all creation reveals the glory of God. This battle of worldviews would seem to imply that apologetic exchange is inevitable within scientific discourse.

We ought also to expect success as we seek to defend the Christian story over against the competing stories of secularized science. Without erring on the side of triumphalism (and given the exceedingly humble state of Christianity in the Western university it is hard to imagine triumphalism among Christian academics!), we may be encouraged by the optimistic tone of Scripture itself. Genesis 3:15, "the earliest foreshadowing of the gospel," "is couched in the language of conquest."[33] The seed of the woman would crush the serpent's head. God mobilized his armies for the conquest of Canaan. In Acts, the gospel spreads from Jerusalem, to Samaria, to the end of the earth. One benefit of foregrounding the antithesis is that we keep in mind God's mission to bring the gospel to every tribe, including psychology.

---

32. Chaplin, *Herman Dooyeweerd*, 61. See also Clouser for a detailed discussion of non-reductive theorizing. Examples of such methods already exist within psychology, these concerns regarding reductionism notwithstanding. See, for example, Sheldon, *Optimal Human Being.*

33. Letham, *Holy Trinity*, 34.

Antithesis does not imply world-flight—just the opposite. We do not leave those lost in unbelief to perish in unbelief. Neither do we leave disciplines mired in unbelief to falter in that unbelief. We must invite these disciplines, as David Powlison puts it, to "intelligent repentance."[34] In the context of academic work, this also inevitably leads us to the question of apologetics.

In engaging psychology with an apologetic edge, we are not asking psychology to change its game. Contemporary psychology is inherently apologetic in the sense that it aims to provide a compelling and coherent understanding of mind and behavior given a particular set of (empiricist and naturalistic) worldview assumptions. Though these assumptions are not usually explicitly stated, we must not be naïve about the fact that in a science like psychology, what is being offered is more than a simple account of "just the facts," but also a story that is thought to render these facts intelligible. God's missional mindset requires Christians to embrace this apologetic side to the discipline.

Typically, if Christians engage in apologetic dialogue in science, they do so from an "evidentialist" strategy. As the term indicates, the facts of the science of psychology would be arranged in such a way as to show the reasonableness of Christian faith. Since God reveals himself through his creation, we ought to expect to encounter plenty of evidences for the faith, and so this strategy would certainly have much to commend it. The problem, however, is that evidentialist approaches tend to forget that their unbelieving interlocutors are not neutral with regard to the truth of Christianity. The antithesis shapes apologetic discourse powerfully—such that, again, as Paul put it, the truth of God clearly revealed in creation is suppressed in unrighteousness (Rom 1:18–20). Apart from the grace of God, those who begin in intellectual autonomy will end in intellectual autonomy. The problem with a simple evidentialist approach is that it does not explicitly challenge this suppressive tendency.

A useful alternative approach to apologetics is "presuppositional." Such an approach recognizes that the way one weighs

---

34. Powlison, "Biblical Counseling View," in *Four Views*, 209.

evidences depends powerfully upon the presuppositions and ultimate commitments that one brings to the exchange. A presuppositional apologetic therefore foregrounds these (often previously implicit) commitments and probes their explanatory adequacy. In my teaching of psychological science, I utilize a two-step argument based upon the apologetics of Cornelius Van Til:

> In our dialogue [with mainstream psychological science] we first for the sake of argument assume that the naturalistic, evolutionary worldview [so widely employed within psychology] is true; that is, we put on naturalistic, evolutionary eyeglasses, so to speak. We then attempt to give a full accounting of the facts and successful (micro-) theories of psychology from this perspective—we ask, "Does the naturalistic, evolutionary worldview—particularly its theory of natural selection building upon unguided but fortuitous genetic mutations—make sense of phenomenon or theory x?" Does human language, for example, or our capacity to discriminate approximately one million shades of color, or our tendency to self-justify, or our disproportionally enormous brain size relative to other species make sense given this worldview and its chosen mechanism of explanation? We also ask, do the assumptions of science itself (such as the reliability of human reason and the regularity and lawfulness of nature) make sense given this worldview? Do things come into focus when we wear these eyeglasses? . . . Then, we ask our "empiricist" interlocutors "for the sake of argument" to assume the truth of Christianity, to put on Scriptural eyeglasses. We ask the same question. Does human language, or our tendency to self-justify, and so on, make sense given the Christian worldview? Do the assumptions of science itself fit within this worldview?[35]

I have been utilizing this approach in my teaching for the last seven years, and I believe that it has three strengths. First, it balances antithesis and common grace. The reality of common grace is affirmed by maintaining that the (well-established) findings of empirical psychology cannot be dismissed but must instead be engaged and interpreted. The antithesis is maintained by challenging the adequacy of the autonomous and naturalistic

---

35. Kosits, "Redeeming Psychology Means Developing an Apologetic Edge," 42.

framework of interpretation.[36] Second, it grants to psychological science the independence and legitimacy that it needs to flourish by distinguishing proximate-level and ultimate-level explanations (more on this below). Third, the approach makes intuitive sense.[37] When accounting for things like awe, language, and music, we compare the frankly strained explanations[38] of Darwinism to the simple fit afforded by the Christian worldview. Therefore, this is the fourth question that should be asked of any attempt to relate psychological science to Christianity—does this approach try to make an apologetic point? If so, does it employ evidentialist, presuppositional, or some combination of these approaches?

Whose Psychology?
Thus far I have argued that defining what we mean by "Christianity" can lead to greater clarity and transparency in any discussion of the relation of psychology and Christianity. Another major source of confusion in the discussion is the term "psychology" itself. Lay people tend to associate the word with therapy or counseling. Historically and etymologically, however, psychology has referred to the systematic study of the soul or the mind. What is the structure of the mind? What are its main

---

36. It is of course also true that an autonomous and naturalistic framework will oftentimes give a particular shape to the proximate-level findings of empirical psychology, and this deserves more attention than I can give it here. Yet, since empirical psychological findings are public knowledge (i.e., they are replicable events) they still must be afforded a high degree of respect.

37. That is, intuitive sense *to Christians* and also to those non-Christians who are able, for the sake of argument and empathy, to try on the interpretive lenses of the Christian worldview. Some non-Christians (usually the less tolerant ones) are unwilling and/or unable to look at reality through Christian eyes, however.

38. There are many areas where Darwinian explanations are not strained, but rather question-begging. "Adaptive" psychological or behavioral phenomena are regularly portrayed as proof of Darwinism. But Darwin co-opted the word "adaptation" from natural *theology* (see Browne, *Darwin's Origin of Species*, 17). In other words, adaptations *used* to be seen as evidence of God. To assume that adaptations necessarily favor Darwinian theory therefore begs the question.

functions? How does the mind work? Take, for example, the first North American college textbook with the word "psychology" in the title, written by Frederick Rauch, published in 1840. The book dealt with topics such as consciousness, sensation, attention, memory, cognition, emotion, and choice.[39] This tradition of inquiry continues today and its most prevalent and obvious incarnation is the introductory psychology course offered by psychology departments worldwide.[40] The "view" that I will advocate in this paper presupposes *this* psychology (though it certainly has implications for other psychologies).

Though psychologists have long entertained an interest in abnormal mental functioning, therapy and counseling are newer phenomena, with separate genealogies. Further, though Freud pioneered his "talking cure" in the late nineteenth and early twentieth centuries, it wasn't until the Second World War that therapy began to gain prominence in psychology. In response to the enormous number of traumatized soldiers, the US government invested funds in the training of clinical psychologists— who had previously been in the business of administering psychological tests but who would now attempt to help the traumatized to recover.[41] Today, the number of psychologists engaged in providing therapy and other human services far exceeds the number of psychologists actively engaged with the traditional disciplinary questions. Hence, the association between the term psychology and the idea of therapy is not unfounded. Certainly therapy and counseling are now incredibly important parts of psychology, but these concerns *are* profoundly different from the classic disciplinary concerns of psychology and the

---

39. Rauch, *Psychology*. Instead of the term "cognition" Rauch referred to "thinking," and the topic of choice was included in his discussion of "the will." This shows that though the terminology of psychology changes to some extent over time (though less than you might think), the content of the discipline has continuity.

40. Though new topics have been added (such as the brain), the old topics covered by authors like Rauch continue to be explored in the Introduction to Psychology course. A superficial inspection of the table of contents of a contemporary introductory psychology textbook will attest to this.

41. Benjamin, *Brief History of Modern Psychology*, 163.

connection between science and therapy is often quite thin.[42] Therefore, if a third edition of *Psychology & Christianity* is published, I would recommend two separate volumes, one with the original title, and another with the title, *Counseling & Christianity*.[43] It will serve the reader well to keep these distinctions in mind as we proceed.

Theoretical Activity in Psychology: Still, psychology proper and therapy and counseling do have more than a few things in common. Both are involved (at least to some extent) in theoretical activity, and a focus on this activity can help to frame the issues at stake. Admittedly, the subject matter of psychology sometimes exceeds the capacities of human language; we often know more in a pre-theoretical way than we can articulate theoretically—a dynamic that is especially observable in therapy. Psychology, however, is an attempt to put into propositional language the dynamic mysteries of the mind. So, while we admit the limitations of theory, we should also recognize that, if we really want to play the game of psychology, we shall inevitably enter into the domain of propositions and theory.

We must, therefore, have some sense of how psychological theory works in mainstream practice. Let me briefly sketch out how it works in the abstract, and then illustrate the phenomenon in a particular area of psychological science. In brief, theoretical activity in psychological science is a multi-level phenomenon,

---

42. Consider this: when the discipline of psychology finally got the couch in the 1940s, it was in a strongly neo-behaviorist phase in which truth claims had to be subjected to the most rigorous empirical test. Yet the theory of psychotherapy that was widely embraced by psychologists then was Freudian! Freud's theories had been held by psychology at arm's-length up to this point because they were perceived to be unscientific. Psychology's embrace of Freud for psychotherapy in the 1940s, then, was not due to science, which illustrates the point. See Benjamin, *Brief History of Modern Psychology*, 144, 164. The recent call within psychology for evidence-based treatments also reflects this reality (though providing evidence for the effectiveness of a particular therapy is still a far cry from deriving a therapy from science).

43. Interestingly, IVP has just released a volume titled *Counseling and Christianity: Five Approaches*, edited by Stephen P. Greggo and Timothy A. Sisemore (2012).

taking place along a proximate/ultimate continuum. At the most proximate level we have the "data" of individual studies, public and replicable construction-observations. One step up from that level we have proximate-level attempts to explain "how" the observed phenomenon works, i.e., the attempt to elucidate psychological or other types of "mechanisms." We may call these "micro-theories." The next, the "meta-theoretical" level, is more integrative, attempting to summarize massive amounts of scientific literature in order to make more general statements about human mind and behavior. Finally, we enter into the realm of explicit or implicit worldview beliefs or stories, which have a pervasive but usually unacknowledged influence on psychological theory because of the claimed demarcation line between facts and values. See Figure A below.

Figure A: The general structure of theory in psychological science

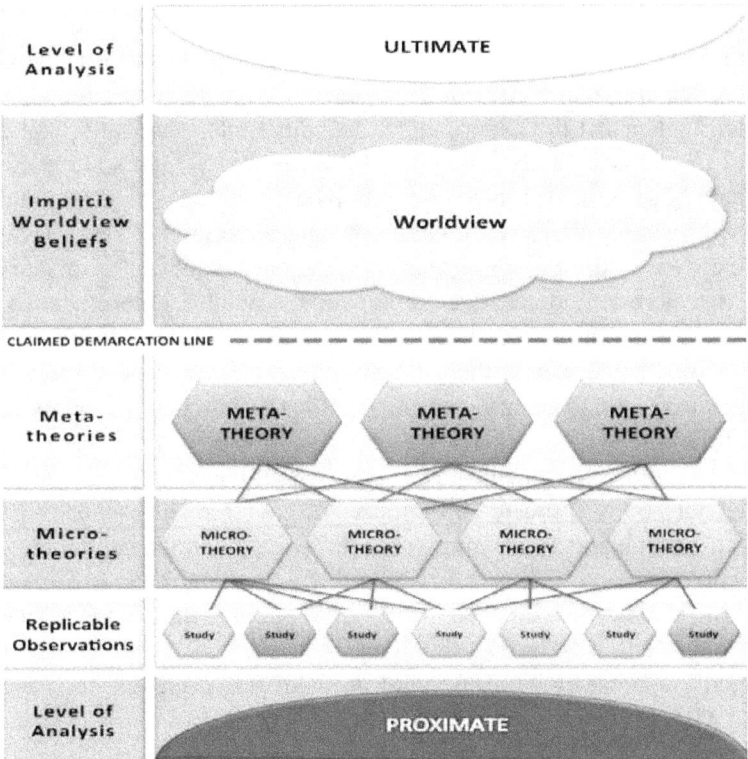

Let me now use the domain of cognitive dissonance research—a topic in the scientific sub-discipline of social psychology—as a concrete example. Again, we can conceptualize psychological theory as a multi-level phenomenon. The most proximate level of analysis is also the most public, having to do with the empirical realities described in scientific articles (or experienced in therapeutic exchange). Empirical research articles are the best example of this level of psychological work. The seminal article in the field of cognitive dissonance research was published in 1959 by Leon Festinger and James Carlsmith.[44] In this study, research participants were subjected to a tediously boring experimental task—of turning knobs again and again, and then placing blocks in a tray, dumping them out of a tray, and placing them back in the tray. In one condition of the experiment, participants were simply asked how they felt about the experiment. (They found it boring.) In two other conditions, the experimenter asked the participants to lie to the next participant (really a person in cahoots with the experimenter), telling her that the experiment was really quite interesting. Some of these participants induced to lie were paid $1 and some were paid $20. Which of these two groups do you think would end up feeling more positive about the boring experiment? Behavioral theory would predict that the bigger reward would be associated with more attitude change—that people would feel more positive feelings about the experiment if they were paid more to lie. But cognitive dissonance theory—which turned out to be correct—made the opposite prediction, the idea being that lying about one's true feelings about the experiment (i.e., saying that they found the experiment interesting when they really found it terribly boring) created an unpleasant feeling of dissonance that the participants were motivated to reduce. Those participants who were paid $20 (a lot of money fifty years ago) had sufficient justification for lying—as if to say, "Well, in reality I thought the experiment was boring, but they paid me $20 so of course I lied!"). Those participants paid only $1, however, did not have

---

44. Festinger and Carlsmith, "Cognitive Consequences."

sufficient justification for their actions. Since they could not take back the lie, there was only one way to reduce dissonance—to change their attitudes toward the experiment. This is precisely what happened. The attitude scores in the $20 and control conditions were negative—the experiment was boring and the participants said so. But in the $1 condition, participants reported that they had positive feelings about the study.

The empirical "objectivity" of this experiment lies in its replicability.[45] If a psychologist desired, she could (with ethics approval) enact the same procedure and observe the same or very similar results.[46] The public nature of such studies is one of the great strengths of a scientific approach to psychology, and its greatest protection from slipping into mere opinion. In counseling there is a data-level analogy in the nitty-gritty interchanges that take place during a therapeutic session. But these data—though in many ways richer and more important—do not share the same "public" and replicable qualities. Hence, a greater degree[47] of subjectivity and interpretation always enters into "the data" of a clinical encounter (though a good therapist will always do her best to listen well before interpreting).[48]

Within psychological science, however, we can make a cleaner distinction between data-level activity and theoretical activity (though the distinction still is not air-tight). All empirical articles describe what happened (and, presumably, what would happen again if replicated). Theory attempts to account for what is observed on a variety of more or less integrative levels. Again, at the most proximate level, psychologists use what we might call "micro-theories" to account for a narrow range of scientific data,

---

45. "Today ... nobody believes that scientists can separate themselves from their already-existing attitudes, and to be objective does not mean to be devoid of such normal human traits. Rather, an objective observation, as the term is used in science, is simply one that can be verified by more than one observer" (Goodwin, *Research in Psychology*, 11). As these verifications or "replications" occur, confidence in a finding is increased.
46. The finding that people will change their attitudes to reduce dissonance has been replicated many times.
47. This is not to say that replicable events are entirely free from theory.
48. Storr, *Freud*, 119.

and these are clearly evidenced in the realm of cognitive dissonance theory. For example, the dissonance that Festinger and Carlsmith induced can be explained as being due to mere inconsistency between cognitions (Festinger's own theory). But this same dissonance may have arisen because of discrepancies between the self concept ("I am the kind of person who tells the truth") and action ("I lied")—the "self-consistency" approach to dissonance research. Another approach, the so-called "new look" theory, posits that dissonance arises when people feel responsible for producing foreseeable aversive consequences ("Boy, I lied about the experiment and now that student is going to be confused and bored!"). Then there is the "self-affirmation" theory, which holds that people feel dissonance when their self-worth is threatened through acts that challenge their sense of moral integrity. I do not intend to debate the worth of these theories at this stage but only desire to illustrate how "micro-theories" work in the field of psychology.[49]

At the next level we have "meta-theories." I use this term in the way that psychologists Roy Baumeister and Mark Leary[50] use it, as a theory that integrates a broad variety of research findings in order to make a more general statement about psychological functioning. Whereas micro-theories explain only a very narrow band of experience, meta-theories are broader, yet still grounded in empirical observations. Baumeister and Leary do a masterful job of integrating massive amounts of empirical literature to argue that human beings have a "need to belong," which simply means that we function best when we have close relationships characterized by loving concern and frequent interaction. In my own introductory psychology class I have argued over the years—in a manner consistent with social psychologists Carol Tavris and Elliot Aronson[51]—that human beings also have

---

49. For a wonderfully concise summary of these micro-theories, see Harmon-Jones and Mills, "Introduction to Cognitive Dissonance Theory."

50. Baumeister and Leary, "Need to Belong."

51. Tavris and Aronson, *Mistakes Were Made*. See also Goethals, "Dissonance and Self-Justification."

a "need"[52] or are *wired for* justification—we hence desire and tend to see ourselves in a positive moral light. Cognitive dissonance phenomena can be related to this broader meta-theory.[53]

Psychological science as it exists today becomes increasingly ambivalent as theoretical explanations become more integrative or general. Baumesiter and Leary acknowledge this in their article on the need to belong, saying that contemporary psychologists "have shown a pervasive reluctance to entertain sweeping generalizations and broad hypotheses,"[54] suggesting that even their painstakingly-researched and highly-documented theory pushes the limits of acceptability within the field of psychological science.

We might, then, be tempted to think of psychology as a purely inductive science, unwilling to venture into speculations when it comes to its work. This would be the wrong conclusion. Though it is true that psychological science is based in large measure upon solid, empirical study, "sweeping generalizations and broad hypotheses" do routinely enter into psychological explanation at an even more ultimate worldview level, particularly in the form of speculations concerning the evolutionary origins of the subject matter. Researchers are free to go beyond the data, beyond micro- and even meta-theoretical statements, and speculate as to the "ultimate" (i.e., Darwinian) significance of whatever they are studying. We needn't go beyond Baumeister and Leary to observe this pervasive tendency: The need to belong, they argue, "presumably has an evolutionary basis. It seems clear that a desire to maintain and to form social bonds

---

52. This is not the place to address the problematics of "need" theories, though Christians ought to be cautious if they are to employ them. See, for example, Welch, "Who Are We?" I do think that the traditional Reformational notion of aspects of functioning provides a helpful way of re-conceiving the issue—humans do not flourish as well as they might when they are not functioning as designed in each modality. Conversely, however, a person may function well within many modalities and still be estranged from God—such a person cannot in an ultimate sense be said to be flourishing.

53. Indeed, the self-consistency approach of Aronson may also be portrayed as a meta-theory; see Aronson, "Return of the Repressed."

54. Baumeister and Leary, "Need to Belong," 498.

Figure B: The structure of theory in psychological science as it currently exists, using cognitive dissonance theory as an example

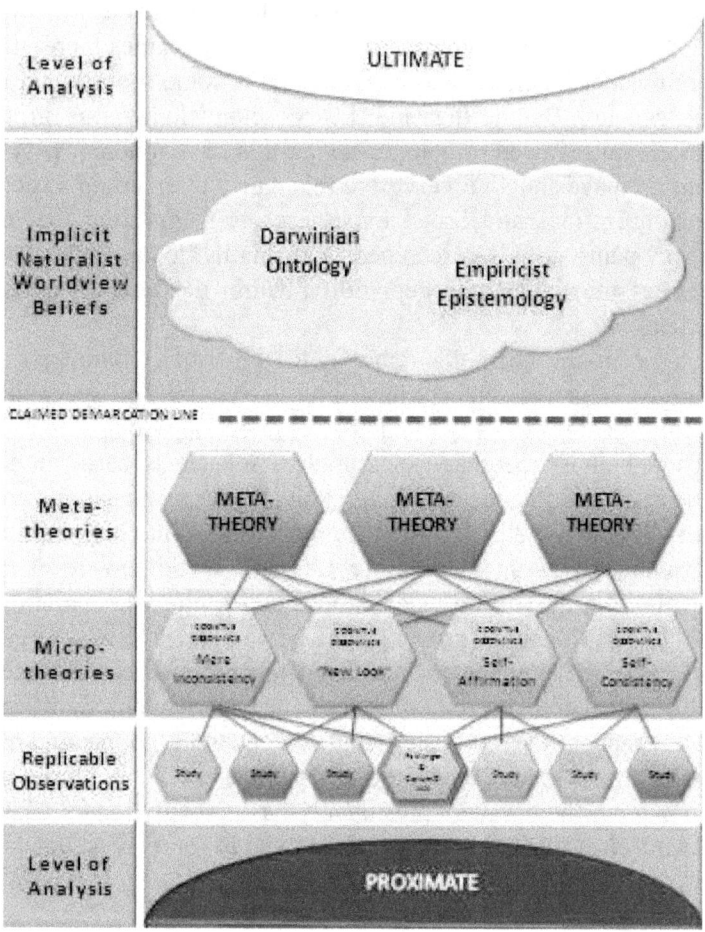

would have both survival and reproductive benefits."[55] Likewise, if we posit a "need for justification" as a meta-theory to explain dissonance phenomena, it would be acceptable within current scientific practice to speculate as to its Darwinian basis. See Figure B.

---

55. Ibid., 499.

It is initially surprising that a discipline that is purportedly allergic to sweeping generalizations and broad hypotheses so regularly uses a sweeping and broad Darwinian worldview to interpret its hard-won findings. This is not to enter into the overly simplified "creation-evolution" debate, which is probably more of a red herring and distraction than we tend to admit or realize. The issue is that psychological science does indeed allow researchers to go well "beyond the data" and engage in ultimate/worldview-level theorizing, so long as that theorizing gives the ultimacy to evolution by undirected natural selection.[56] Natural selection has within science today the status of a "divinity belief," a status that goes well beyond the evidence.[57] Any perspective that gives *ultimacy* to a created thing is, the reader should recall, idolatrous, setting itself up against the

---

56. I should add that Darwin's theory of sexual selection is occasionally added to the mix to explain "extravagant" features like peacocks' tails or, in the case of psychology, human mental abilities, which "look too excessive and expensive to have evolved for survival" (Miller, *The Mating Mind*, 11).

57. This is illustrated powerfully in Richard Dawkins polemic against belief in God, in which he replaces God with natural selection, which "explains the whole of life" (Dawkins, *The God Delusion*, 116). In the realm of psychological science it is unusual to find micro-theories that can explain so much, but naturalists like Dawkins insist that, in the realm of biology, undirected natural selection *must* explain "apparent" design in nature because there is no other known natural process that can. "I have yet to meet a serious biologist who can point to an alternative to natural selection as a driving force of *adaptive* evolution" (Dawkins, *Greatest Show on Earth*, 18). Since there is no alternative, it *must* be natural selection. Though I respect Dawkins immensely for his passionate eloquence, intelligence, and love of the natural world, the fallacy here is obvious. The evidence for undirected natural selection's omnipotence is extremely weak. It is, for example, the weak link in Jerry Coyne's impressive array of evidence for evolution (Coyne, *Why Evolution Is True*, see ch. 5, "The Engine of Evolution"). But without undirected natural selection, the secular establishment simply does not know "what evolution is," to borrow from Ernst Mayr's phrase. In emphasizing the limitations of *undirected* natural selection, I follow Plantinga, *Where the Conflict Really Lies*, 12. For a sustained attempt to discuss the limits of natural selection (and should we not be able to talk about the limits of *any* scientific theory?) see: Behe, *Edge of Evolution*. My sense is that within mainstream psychological science it is simply assumed that natural selection is an undirected process. The notion of "divinity belief," is, of course, Roy Clouser's.

knowledge of God.[58] Only God is ultimate, and ultimate-level theorizing that neglects this fact will inevitably distort and err.

There are at least three possible ways to deal with the reality of ultimate-level sense-making in psychological science. One option, the least desirable of all, is to continue current practice without reflection. Another option would be to buckle down and insist that telling such "just-so stories" is illegitimate within scientific discourse.[59] Given that the ultimate-proximate level distinction is here to stay within psychological science,[60] however, this seems highly unlikely. The other much more difficult path—the one I advocate—is to identify ultimate-level sense-making for what it is—a way of bringing worldview-level beliefs into the interpretive game of psychological science. When this is identified as such, other worldview beliefs should be given an interpretive chance.[61] But this pathway is difficult because of the perception that Darwinian stories, since they are stories of unguided material causation, are "scientific," while theistic stories, because they are stories that may involve non-material causation, are not scientific. But stories are stories—the question is *which one makes best sense of what we see and what we assume and what we do in psychological science?* My claim is that Christian theism does it best.

Therefore, the fifth and final question that should be asked of any attempt to relate psychology and Christianity is: How does it conceptualize psychological theory? Does it attempt to balance both proximate and ultimate-levels of theorizing, or does it

---

58. This is not to say that Christians in psychology cannot avoid idolatry. My sense is that many Christians in psychology privately interpret evolutionary statements in psychological science as presupposing God, or simply dismiss the statements altogether.

59. Jerry Coyne's criticism of evolutionary psychology is typical (Coyne, *Why Evolution Is True*, 228).

60. In psychology, "natural selection is uncontroversially an ultimate source of explanation" (Scott-Phillips, Dickins, and West, "Evolutionary Theory," 43). This particular article, appearing in one of the discipline's more high-profile venues, argues that the distinction is useful, but also frequently misapplied.

61. Here I would employ a modified version of George Marsden's advocacy of a true pluralism within the "secular" academy. See Marsden, *Outrageous Idea*, ch. 3.

emphasize one or the other? Is it aware of the way ultimate-level commitments routinely creep into psychological science?

A Pair of Prevailing Perspectivalisms

The position I am advocating here has been influenced powerfully by the first edition of *Psychology & Christianity*, yet is a bit different from the positions described in that book. As I see it, the positions advocated in the first edition—*particularly when viewed from the vantage point of their usefulness in engaging psychological science*[62]—may be reduced to two "perspectivalisms," one modern, the other postmodern, to employ two overworked terms. Modern perspectivalism is strong in its (implicit) affirmation of common grace, but weak in its (implicit) denial of the antithesis. Similarly, modern perspectivalism is strong in its commitment to carefully and accurately read the book of God's works, nature (particularly human nature), but weak in its neglect of Scripture. Further, modern perspectivalism has a preference for micro-theories, bio-psycho-social aspects of human functioning, and a penchant for evidential apologetics.

Postmodern perspectivalism provides the opposite set of concerns. It is strong on antithesis, but weak on common grace, strong on Scripture, but weak on nature. It has a preference for ultimate-level theorizing, a focus on religious (faith-related) aspects of human functioning, and a general neglect of apologetics.

The position I will advocate offers a third perspectivalism that attempts to incorporate the strengths of both approaches, and correct for their shortcomings.

Modern Perspectivalism

The first position described in the book is the "levels of explanation approach" of David G. Myers. Myers is a social psychologist at Hope College in Michigan, the author of some best-selling introduction to psychology and social psychology

---

62. Again, this *is not* the primary purpose of some of the authors, so the critique that I offer is not so much of their position *per se*, but of their adequacy for work in the academic discipline of psychology.

textbooks, and the only psychological scientist in the first edition book. He is also a leading thinker on the relationship between Christianity and psychology, co-authoring, for example, the widely-adopted *Psychology through the Eyes of Faith*.[63] Myers's "levels of explanation" approach, described and applied in these two widely adopted books, has therefore had wide exposure in Christian universities and represents what I believe to be the most common (and common-sense) approach to relating faith to psychological science.

In the 1970s, Christian philosopher C. Stephen Evans described the position advocated by David Myers and those like him as "perspectivalism"[64]—the idea being that each discipline has a valid but limited perspective on reality. If we consider, for example, a phenomenon such as memory,[65] we can look at it from a variety of "levels of explanation." At the broadest and most integrative [most ultimate] level, for example, St. Augustine reflected on the analogies between God's triune nature and the relationship among memory, understanding, and will.[66] Likewise, theologians could systematically study the ways the Scripture itself portrays memory as a barometer of covenantal faithfulness. On the level of philosophy, the interrelationship between memory and personal identity might be explored. Social psychologists look at the influences of mood on memory. Cognitive psychologists sometimes look at memory from a capacity standpoint, studying, for example, how much information people can hold in short-term memory. Biopsychologists might consider the brain regions and neurotransmitters associated with memory. Biochemists may delve into the complex molecular structure of those neurotransmitters. Physicists may be able to explain the general physical laws that govern how these molecules work.

---

63. Myers and Jeeves, *Psychology through the Eyes of Faith*. The first edition of this book appeared in 1987.

64. Evans, "Christian Perspectives," 106–8; Evans, *Preserving the Person*, 105–17.

65. Myers and Jeeves use memory as their key example—I have expanded on it here.

66. Teske, "Augustine's Philosophy of Memory."

The point that "perspectivalists" want to make is a good one—it *is* possible to consider reality from multiple levels of understanding. If one were to ask, "which is the correct level of understanding?" we would dismiss the question as ill-informed. Indeed, the validity of some form of a levels-of-explanation approach seems to be implied by the modal nature of God's providential control of the universe. Fully understanding anything in God's creation requires that we understand how it functions in each modality. So there is something fundamentally *right* about perspectivalism thus defined, and any Christian engagement with psychology will do well to retain this perspective. Indeed, the third perspectival approach that I outline in this article is in some ways an *integrative* levels-of-explanation approach.

The main problem with the levels-of-explanation approach advocated by Myers, however, is its modernity. Years ago historian George Marsden described the "evangelical love affair with Enlightenment science," showing that in the eighteenth and nineteenth centuries, Christians in North America approached the faith-learning question from the vantage point of a "two-tiered worldview."[67] Having adopted a version of the Enlightenment that was at least on the surface of things congenial to Christian faith, North American evangelicals simply assumed that science and faith would always cohere. Since science is objective, there was therefore no need to explicitly inject Christian assumptions into scientific work—a kind of "methodological secularization" took hold. Yet Marsden shows that this methodological secularization eventually morphed into a worldview secularization in which Christian viewpoints were no longer welcome in mainstream science. This is indeed the case in psychological science—we are allowed to *be* Christian, and even to write books on psychology from a Christian vantage point, or to quote the Bible or other Christian sources for broader intellectual context, but we must not insist that the Christian faith or the Christian God has any interpretive authority in scientific work *per se*. Yet, as I have contended above, this is unfair, for other (naturalistic and evolutionary) worldview assumptions

---

67. Marsden, *Understanding Fundamentalism and Evangelicalism*, 131.

have free interpretive rein in psychology. Hence I think it is fair to say that modern perspectivalism is inattentive to the ways these ultimate-level commitments creep—or march!—into the discipline.

A Strong Emphasis on the Book of God's Works: Myers, as a scientist, is strong on creation. The proper posture of a psychologist is to be "humble before nature and skeptical of human authority."[68] He notes that the leaders of the Scientific Revolution arose in a Christian milieu, and that we, like these scientific forerunners, ought to assume that we are dealing with "an intelligible creation," and that we ought to "seek its truths by observing and experimenting." The ideal is "disciplined, rigorous inquiry—checking our theories against reality . . . "[69] Myers is certainly right to take his Christianity as a mandate for open and honest scientific inquiry: "If God is the ultimate author of whatever truth psychological science glimpses, then I can accept that truth, however surprising or unsettling."[70] We ought always to "put testable ideas to the test,"[71] allowing scientific procedures to "clean the cloudy spectacles through which we view the world."[72] He is also certainly right to emphasize that careful attentiveness to God's creation leads to a "sense of awe and wonder."[73]

However, Myers, as a social psychologist, is not nearly as attentive to the book of God's Words. He discusses biblical teaching only insofar as it intersects with the current research concerns and findings of psychological science, and frames the issues in terms of whether the fields are contradictory or compatible. He is right to note that most of proximate-level psychological science is deeply compatible with a biblical view of the world. The asymmetry of his approach is apparent, however, in three main ways. There is first an asymmetry of depth. In

---

68. Myers, "Levels-of-Explanation View," 55.
69. Ibid.
70. Ibid.
71. Ibid., 58.
72. Ibid., 57–58.
73. Ibid., 58.

making the argument for compatibility, he somewhat hastily looks for parallels between the basic findings of social psychology (which he masterfully summarizes)[74] and the basic teachings of Christianity. We are told, for example, that social psychology's affirmation of the need for self-esteem is parallel to the Bible's idea of grace. Though there may be analogies here, the *differences* are more interesting (e.g., grace's devastating blow to moral self esteem). There is further asymmetry in Myer's repeated contention that we ought to put our ideas to the (empirical) test. Why only the *empirical* test? Are there not other tests that would be of interest to a Christian, such as compatibility with Scripture? Finally, Myers's asymmetry of approach is evidenced in that when science and faith appear to contradict, Myers seems to prefer to go back and re-interpret the biblical data, not the natural data, as in the case of homosexuality. In short, the book of God's Works seems to have interpretative primacy over the book of his Words.

A Strong Emphasis on Common Grace with No Sense of Antithesis: With such a strong affirmation of the legitimacy of psychological science, we find in Myers's approach an admirable first-hand sense of the way God's truth pervades the field. He rejects the idea that science and faith are "competing systems of explanation"[75] and instead emphasizes the compatibilities between Scripture and science. However, because Myers does not seem to discern the subtle and not-so-subtle ways unbelieving assumptions pervade psychology, he has little to say that would radically challenge or alter the highly secularized discipline. The current definition of psychology is embraced without comment, and he outlines seven different ways one might relate faith to psychology, none of which suggest that psychology would need to change in any way.[76] Yet, as I have indicated above, the prevailing assumption in the discipline is that one can

---

74. Ibid., 61–65.
75. Ibid., 54.
76. Ibid., 60. The list is nonetheless an extremely useful menu of options for Christians in mainstream contexts.

have an adequate understanding of mind and behavior without making reference to God or Scripture. He is also uncritical of the pervasively naturalistic metaphysics and empiricist epistemology of the discipline. And though Myers is aware that bias can influence scientific work, he tends to interpret this bias as the discipline typically does,[77] in *individualistic* terms, as something that can be weeded out through empirical investigation. The biases of which I speak, however, are part of the sociology of psychological science, part of the worldview of psychological science, and are thus largely invisible and typically unruffled by empirical test.

An Implicit Acceptance of Reductive Explanations: Psychological science embraces three main levels of analysis, the biological, psychological, and social, i.e., the bio-psycho-social approach.[78] This approach, as Myers correctly notes,[79] is not inherently reductionistic but inherent to the nature of scientific inquiry—scientific explanations of necessity must isolate a few variables and make sense of them. Still, if reductionisms are understood to occur when one aspect of God's world is given interpretive primacy, psychological science is still often guilty of reductionisms in two main ways. The first and least concerning of these is that individual psychologists (not Myers) have an understandable tendency to forget that they are dealing with just one or two levels of explanation and act as if their narrow focus is the key that unlocks everything else (recall, for example, Skinner's optimism about reinforcement history). The second of these is much more systematic and pervasive. Again, psychologists today frequently posit Darwinian explanations as ultimate explanations, "We can see how—insert psychological phenomenon here—would have helped our evolutionary forebears survive in an ancestral environment," etc. So it is simply not the

---

77. See, for example, Gerrig et al., *Psychology and Life*, 27.
78. Myers, *Psychology*, 8–9.
79. He explicitly frames his levels of explanation approach as an alternative to reductionism in Myers, *Human Puzzle*, 10–11.

case that psychology does not "answer the ultimate questions,"[80] as Myers claims.[81]

Evidential Apologetics: One can also discern a kind of apologetic in Myers's writings, as has historically been the case for modern perspectivalists.[82] In noting the many "parallels" between the findings of psychological science and the traditional pronouncements of Christian theology, Myers is implicitly claiming that scientific evidence corroborates or provides evidence for Christian faith. Science claims that human beings are unique in their rational capacity and need to explain and predict behavior, yet it has also pointed out the many ways we are "prone to overconfidence" in our thinking. Theology has likewise claimed that "we have dignity but not deity."[83] Psychological science shows that we have a self-serving bias—a tendency to view ourselves positively even when we shouldn't—as well as a need for self-esteem. Myers sees a parallel between these ideas and older religious teachings about pride and the need of human beings for God's grace. Psychological science has also largely corroborated Christian beliefs about the importance of intact families and the benefits of a healthy faith life.

---

80. Myers, "Levels-of-Explanation View," 56.
81. It is interesting, however, that Myers lists "natural selection of adaptive traits" as among the other "biological influences" of behavior, such as genes, brain mechanisms, and hormones. See Myers, *Psychology*, 8. But there is a difference between *observing* brain activity during a memory task using an fMRI, and *speculating* as to the Darwinian cause of that mechanism. One is based on observation, the other is not. This is why evolutionary psychologists readily distinguish between proximate and ultimate explanations, with evolutionary speculations being of the "ultimate" variety. "Proximate questions (explanations) have to do with mechanisms. They are 'plumbing and wiring' explanations, and generally answer 'how?' questions: How does the system work? Ultimate questions (explanations) concern the evolution of the trait. Generally, they answer the question 'why?': Why does this system exist, and why does it have the form it does?" (Gaulin and McBurney, *Evolutionary Psychology*, 15).
82. To use Marsden's language, Myers is in this and other senses a modern-day "Warfieldian" (Marsden, *Understanding Fundamentalism and Evangelicalism*).
83. Myers, "Levels-of-Explanation View," 61.

In 2008, Myers expanded these arguments into a short book[84] in which he argues for the reasonableness of faith on the basis of psychological science. As is the case with all evidential apologetics (based upon the assumption of epistemological autonomy), he presents only a probable case. Further, the book is not necessarily a commendation of Christianity, but an argument for a more general and vague "faith." Nonetheless, with endorsements from prominent atheists Michael Shermer and Jonathan Haidt, Myers is to be commended for so winsomely making a case for faith.

A Preference for Micro-theories: Since theoretical activity in psychological science tends to emphasize micro-level explanations of proximate-level empirical findings, Myers's understanding of psychological theory has this same emphasis. When one of his interlocutors criticizes the personality theory of Alfred Adler, Myers correctly points out that the science of psychology does not pay much attention to such grand, more ultimate-level theories.

Postmodern Perspectivalism
In our contemporary intellectual context, the term "perspectivalism" tends to be used in a more postmodern sense.[85] (It is hence ironic that the term "perspectivalism" is reserved for an essentially modern position in the faith-psychology dialogue). If modern perspectivalism rightly notes that each discipline may offer a valid perspective on reality that does not contradict other levels, postmodern perspectivalism counters with the observation that multiple perspectives are possible within any given level or

---

84. Myers, *Friendly Letter*.
85. Kuklick, "On Critical History," 59, says, "*Perspectivalism* . . . a close kinsperson of postmodernism," is the idea that "competing worldviews are incommensurable and reflect incompatible ways of seeing the world, or even of talking about seeing a world. Christians—as well as perhaps feminists, Afrocentrists, gays and lesbians—may have insights that are irreducible to those of others, and experience has shown us that there is no rational way to adjudicate among such *Weltanschauungen*."

discipline. Psychology is not a theoretically unified field.[86] Are we talking about functional or structural psychology, behavioral or gestalt, humanist, feminist, evolutionary, cultural, community, Buddhist, or Roman Catholic? Certainly these various schools will often offer complementary truths. But just as often they will likely offer conflicting perspectives.

It is also the case that history, personal and institutional bias, professional training and standards, and a variety of other factors will tend to institutionalize one or two of these perspectives and rule others out.[87] Progress in the sociology of science has made these points crystal clear. The work of Thomas Kuhn—now fifty years old—powerfully drove home the idea that "normal science" always operates within "paradigms."[88] Historian of psychology Kurt Danziger applied these insights to the discipline of psychology, showing that psychology always operates within a variety of "social contexts of investigative practice," which include the "prevailing standards of what constitutes scientific psychological knowledge."[89] David Leary, another historian of

---

86. Or as Powlison, "Biblical Counseling View," 197, puts it, "There is no unitary psychology." To be fair, however, we do need to concede that contemporary psychological science is unified in several ways, primarily in its admirable "commitment to a *scientific* psychology" (Gleitman, Reisberg, and Gross, *Psychology*, 13). Still, as my historical examples illustrate, this commitment to empiricism has not produced a unified psychology. Another line of argumentation in support of this contention is the substantial mainstream literature on the "unification of psychology." For perhaps the most high-profile contribution to this literature see Sternberg, *Unity in Psychology*. The great appeal of evolutionary psychology in recent years is also undoubtedly tied to its ability to deal with the "theoretical disarray" of psychological science. See Buss, "Evolutionary Psychology," 1.

87. Powlison, "Biblical Counseling View," 215, 217, notes that "ideas and practices do not exist in a vacuum; they happen somewhere," pointing out that institutionalization runs through educational programs, clinics, licensing laws, insurance companies, publishers, and drug companies. "Power is wielded because theories and therapies are institutionalized." He further reiterates the excellent postmodern insight that psychology can be considered "a system of institutional arrangements," and that these institutions "are not givens of the natural order."

88. Kuhn, *Structure of Scientific Revolutions*.

89. Danziger, *Constructing the Subject*, 7, 11.

psychology, has argued persuasively that the history of psychology can be understood as a series or array of different metaphors, and, indeed that all scientific work—psychological or otherwise—is inevitably metaphorical.[90]

For good reason, then, many Christian thinkers have embraced these postmodern insights, and have sought to forge Christian perspectives within the field, to shape "our own distinctive psychology."[91] Believers are charged to take every thought captive to the obedience of Christ, so such an approach seems necessary and worthwhile. Nevertheless, the shortcoming of embracing these insights is that they have a distinctly relativistic sound to them. Is Christianity really just another "paradigm" or set of "biases," or is it *the* Paradigm of paradigms?

For the last seven or so years, I have portrayed the other two approaches that I have found useful and attractive in the first edition of *Psychology & Christianity*, the "Biblical Counseling View," and the "Christian Psychology View," as "postmodern perspectivalist" approaches. Before I explain why I have portrayed these viewpoints as "postmodern," allow me to provide a brief overview of both approaches.

The "Biblical Counseling View" of David Powlison and his colleagues is concerned primarily with applying the gospel of God's grace in Christ to everyday struggles such as anxiety and worry, depression, marital struggles, fear of man, etc., believing that the gospel is the power of God, the only means to truly radical change in a human personality. The movement began as a conservative Christian variety of the antipsychiatry movement of the 1960s, and has developed into a flourishing ministry that has helped many Christians mature, including myself. The concern of the movement is primarily pastoral, and through its hub in Philadelphia, the Christian Counseling and Educational Foundation, it trains ministers and lay people to help themselves and others deal with their struggles in a Christ-centered way. As such, the movement is not *primarily* concerned with how to relate Christianity to the academic discipline of psychology *per*

---

90. Leary, "Psyche's Muse."
91. Powlison, "Biblical Counseling View," 222.

se. For this reason, I am conscious of the fact that my criticisms of the movement are not entirely fair. I am asking very different questions. I am concerned with how—as a confessionally Reformed Christian—to engage the academic discipline of scientific psychology. They are primarily concerned about how the gospel changes people.[92]

Arguably, the key insight of the Christian Psychology approach of Robert Roberts is that, if one embraces a broad enough definition of "psychology," it becomes clear that Christians have long been engaged in the enterprise. Like the humanists of old, Roberts's charge is *ad fontes!*, back to the original Christian sources of psychological insight. The major task of Christian Psychology is to "retrieve the Christian psychology of the past," by allowing the old sources to speak for themselves (without imposing a foreign, modernistic psychological framework upon them) yet also translating these older works into language that we can recognize as psychology. The promise of Christian Psychology, Roberts argues, is that as contemporary Christians in the discipline become familiar with older Christian visions of the person, they may be set free from the distorting cognitive shackles of "establishment psychology."

I have tremendous respect for Powlison and Roberts (as I do for Myers) and am convinced that they both have made seminal contributions to our shared goal of developing an authentically Christian psychology. I have (imperfectly!) incorporated the insights of Powlison and his colleagues into my own personal walk with Christ, as well as into my occasional preaching and practical theological work. I have been emboldened by Roberts's Christian Psychology approach to have students study Jonathan Edwards's *Religious Affections* in my history of psychology class. And I recently asked both of these men, alongside David

---

[92]. "We should not simply ask, 'Is this the correct view,' but rather turn that question into a more flexible, conditional one: 'Is this a good view for understanding how my Christian faith relates *given this . . . setting . . .*'" i.e., as a teacher of psychological science (Johnson, "Gaining Understanding," 298). For a representative and "big picture" overview, see Lane and Tripp, *How People Change*. The book begins with a tribute to Powlison as the father of the contemporary Biblical Counseling Movement.

Myers and others, to participate in a symposium I edited on the topic of "Redeeming Psychology."[93] My criticisms of the viewpoints espoused in the first edition of *Psychology & Christianity* come from my own context, that of a university professor, charged with teaching "secular" psychological science from a faithfully Christian vantage point. It is when one looks at the viewpoints of Powlison and Roberts in *this* context that the shortcomings of their approaches become evident.

It is also from this vantage point of psychology professor that the chapters by Powlison and Roberts begin to feel a little "postmodern." In one sense this is not fair at all to characterize these seminal thinkers as postmodern, because they are not relativistic or radically postmodern in their own thinking. But I have used this term for two primary reasons. The first is to remind my students that additional thought is needed—psychology departments at Christian universities could never simply adopt either position *as is*. We need to do more than simply develop a distinctively Christian view of persons; we need also to show that Christian psychology is not true for Christians only, but that a truly Christian psychology will be a universally true psychology (and to its credit mainstream psychology is still in the business of making universal truth claims). Second, the term fits because Powlison and Roberts do employ certain (valid and important) postmodern insights.

By virtue of their academic training alone, we might expect to see a more postmodern edge to their work. Roberts writes as a philosopher, and philosophers have long seen past the veneer of simple or unnuanced objective truth claims.[94] It is important to note that Powlison's PhD is in the history and sociology of science, a discipline highly attuned to the ways in which science

---

93. Myers wrote, "Redeeming Psychology Means Taking Psychological Science Seriously." Powlison wrote, "Redeeming Psychology Means Learning How to Better Use the Bible in Psychological Work." Roberts wrote, "Redeeming Psychology Means Recovering the Christian Psychology of the Past."

94. This is especially true of Christian philosophers. For a sustained refutation of the modern epistemological project, written by a Christian philosopher, see Wolterstorff, *Reason within the Bounds of Religion*.

falls short of its modernist rhetoric of objectivity and neutrality. It is therefore no wonder that Powlison's original essay employs many of the useful "postmodern" concepts originating in the sociology of science. For example, he argues that theory not only "selects facts based on what it has determined to be significant,"[95] but that:

> all observations are constructed to a degree, but some observations may be pure artifacts. A theory tells us that certain things "have to be there"; the eye fills in the details wittingly or unwittingly. Sometimes people make things up. Research data is notoriously fluid and liable to be fudged; clinicians most often see what they expect to see. Sometimes dubious facts arise from complicity by the subjects studied . . . Sometimes bogus facts arise from biases built into testing instruments . . . In each case the fabrication may be calculated, but more often it simply just happens.[96]

In what follows, I will attempt to situate Powlison and Roberts's essays within the theological and philosophical framework described in the beginning of this essay.

An Emphasis on the Book of God's Words: Perhaps it goes without saying that the biblical counseling approach of David Powlison puts an emphasis on the Scriptures. We are to turn to the Scriptures for a summary of "the Faith's psychology," and "our own 'psychology' will flourish" as we, for example, "unfold Ephesians 3:14–5:2 afresh."[97] Still, in this chapter Powlison says little about how we might derive a psychology from Scripture, the role of tradition, or the distinctively Reformed notion of faith within which he works.

The Christian Psychology approach of Robert Roberts is a bit different—less clinically-oriented than Powlison, and more philosophical and theoretical. Still, the emphasis is on the Scriptures, or on Christian tradition (an emphasis that involves interpretation of Scripture). Roberts argues that a distinctively Christian psychology ought "in large part" to aim to "retrieve the Christian

---

95. Powlison, "Biblical Counseling View," 201.
96. Ibid., 202.
97. Ibid., 221.

psychology of the past,"[98] contained in authors such as Augustine, Aquinas, Edwards, Kierkegaard, and Dostoyevsky. The Scriptures are for Roberts "the fountainhead of Christian ideas, including psychological ones." Therefore, "much of the foundational work in Christian psychology" will include "the careful reading of Scripture."[99] Indeed, the longest section of Roberts's chapter is an exegesis explicating the "Christian psychology" of Matthew 5. Roberts does seem a bit more interested in scientific research than Powlison, but only in those areas having to do directly with religion. He would find important the study of "the impact of religious commitment on the healthiness or unhealthiness of mental and social functioning,"[100] for example.

A Strong Sense of Antithesis and Ambivalence toward Non-Christian Insight: David Powlison and I embrace the same theological tradition, so it should not be surprising that the themes of antithesis and common grace pervade his essay. The emphasis in this chapter, however, clearly falls on the antithesis.

There are phrases in Powlison's essay that indicate an open-mindedness to secular ways of thought. "How then should we view psychological information? Bring it on . . . "[101] "With a careful caveat about the theory-ladenness of data and with a well-trained ability to think from our own point of view (Heb 5:14), we can learn from and interact with anything."[102] He even concedes that " . . . at their best, [psychologists] know a great deal about people,"[103] and affirms the insights of various secular thinkers. "Freud's observational and narrative abilities," for example, "are dazzling."[104]

Still, his affirmations of common grace in this chapter are tepid. For example, he affirms that non-Christian theorists are assisted by "God's providential common grace *scattering* bless-

98. Roberts, "Christian Psychology View," 153.
99. Ibid., 159.
100. Ibid., 170.
101. Powlison, "Biblical Counseling View," 204.
102. Ibid.
103. Ibid., 199.
104. Ibid., 202.

ings and restraining evils,"[105] and that there are "*instances* of good sense and insight . . . *scattered* in psychology books."[106]

Powlison's sense of antithesis, on the other hand, is strong and unambiguous. "Sinners theorize sinfully about sinners."[107] For Christians, "our theistic rational system is directly opposed by naturalistic rational systems,"[108] and "all [within secular psychology] agree that human beings are autonomous rather than responsible to an objective God who acts and speaks."[109] These psychologies seem to try to prove that "anything but Christianity's view of things is true."[110] Further, "a perverting dynamic works to undermine even the sharpest observations and best intentions."[111] Unbelieving theories "systematically suppress . . . the truth . . . "[112] "Institutional structures tacitly shape many assumptions that work against the Faith."[113] Hence, because of the distorting "epistemological effects" of unbelief, "we must interact with secular knowledge with an intentional, self-conscious ambivalence . . . "[114]

There is a robust but less keen sense of antithesis in Roberts's essay. A core conviction of Roberts's Christian Psychology view is that secular psychologies have worldview commitments that oppose the Christian worldview. The reason he recommends that we retrieve the Christian psychology of the past, then, is that contemporary psychology "originates in various strands of the Enlightenment and Romantic individualism or science or scientism . . . "[115] One of the major methodological aspects of Christian Psychology is "to read the [Christian psychological] tradition *pure*," which means that we should strive to understand

---

105. Ibid., 213; italics added.
106. Ibid.; italics added.
107. Ibid., 208.
108. Ibid., 209.
109. Ibid., 208.
110. Ibid., 209.
111. Ibid., 203.
112. Ibid., 221.
113. Ibid., 216.
114. Ibid., 203.
115. Roberts, "Christian Psychology View," 149–50.

these older Christian thinkers on their own terms without modern psychology "contaminating"[116] our understanding of the classics. "Thus one aspect of the method of Christian Psychology is prophylactic: It is to bracket the *substance* of twentieth-century psychologies so that we can put the Christian tradition in the psychological driver's seat."[117] To keep a sharp edge, Christian psychologists must "be especially attentive to *differences* between the Christian tradition and twentieth-century psychologies."[118] Because Christianity has its own psychology, and because mainstream contemporary psychology originates in a very different faith commitment, "the measure that we lose touch with our own psychology and replace it with one of the psychologies of the establishment or some conglomeration of them, we will also lose touch with the apostolic faith."[119]

An Emphasis on the Aspects of Faith and Ethics: Powlison is right when he says, "we are innately and thoroughly worshippers."[120] *All* of life is religious, and the minutiae of day-to-day functioning reveal what we truly worship. Nevertheless, both Powlison and Roberts seem to focus on psychological functioning as it relates to what is traditionally called "the religious life," i.e., human relation to God in faith and to others in love.[121] "Life has to do with God," Powlison (correctly) says, and biblical counseling resists any therapeutic intervention that "replace[s] faith in God."[122] Likewise, Roberts's emphasis on the Christian psychology of old theologians and on the empirical study of religion puts the same emphasis on "religion" in this narrower sense, and his explication of the Sermon on the Mount emphasizes the ethical aspect of human life. Now certainly these are admirable emphases that fill a deplorable lacuna in con-

---

116. Ibid., 155.
117. Ibid., 156.
118. Ibid., 157.
119. Ibid., 171.
120. Powlison, "Biblical Counseling View," 219.
121. In Reformational philosophy, these have to do with the pistic (or faith-related) and ethical (love-related) modalities of God's providential control.
122. Powlison, "Biblical Counseling View," 219, 218.

temporary psychological science.[123] Psychological functioning cannot, however, be reduced to its relation to these crucial aspects of faith and ethics. By God's own design, we function in a variety of other ways, and a satisfying and full-orbed Christian psychology would need to deal with the relation of psychological functioning to these other aspects of life too.

An Undeveloped Presuppositional Apologetic: One of the great strengths of Powlison's "biblical counseling" approach is his deep sense of the explanatory power of the Christian worldview, reflecting the Van Tillian origins of the Biblical Counseling Movement. The key to Van Til's presuppositional apologetic was the idea that the Christian worldview uniquely interprets the world. Again and again, Powlison emphasizes this point: "the truth rightly interprets every fact";[124] "only the Faith has a principle by which our tendency to distort can be continually corrected: God's point of view."[125] Borrowing from a Van Tillian analogy, he argues that those who do not see "with the Faith's eyes" necessarily distort the facts, as if operating "a powerful table saw set at a 75-degree angle. When [they] cut . . . a forest into boards, [they] cut . . . every board crooked. But the Faith sees it true; it cuts boards at right angles."[126] But this key apologetic insight is—ironically enough—undeveloped in biblical counseling, though for understandable reasons.[127] The main concern of biblical counselors is overwhelmingly to help Christians learn to live their lives in the light of the riches of Christ's

---

123. Recent investigation in "positive psychology" has begun to address these aspects of functioning from a scientific vantage point.

124. Powlison, "Biblical Counseling View," 201.

125. Ibid., 202.

126. Ibid., 203.

127. I say this underdevelopment is ironic not only because of the Van Tillian origins of biblical counseling, but also because apologetics figures prominently in the curriculum of the CCEF and is one of the main topic areas they use to organize articles published in the *Journal of Biblical Counseling*. But my sense is that the primary aim of these things is not apologetic exchange with non-Christians in psychology, but rather to equip Christians as they encounter secular ideas. Further, as a counseling movement, they understandably do not tend to engage psychological science.

redemption, not to show the explanatory superiority of the Christian worldview in an apologetic interchange with unbelievers. The apologetic of biblical counseling, they have said, is changed lives, and this indeed is the more important apologetic. But for those of us who teach the academic discipline of psychology, the theoretical apologetic must be developed. We must actually *show* that Christian faith does a better job of ultimate-level explanation than does the naturalistic/Darwinian worldview so dominant in contemporary psychology.

I have not discerned an apologetic in Roberts's chapter. Given that he thinks of modern psychology as coming from one faith position, and Christian psychology from another, the implication would seem to be that we are dealing with simple incommensurability. With no meaningful point of contact, apologetic exchange would seem to be out of line.[128] So in practice, neither of our postmodern perspectivalist authors has much to say—in these chapters at least—to the discipline of scientific psychology *per se*.

An Emphasis on Ultimate-level Theories in Psychology: Powlison writes with a keen awareness of the distinction between the "data-level" and the "theory-level" in psychological work. He is certainly right to reiterate the postmodern insight that "psychological knowledge never presents 'just the facts,'" but that "theory has multiple effects on observation and research." Theories select facts, and have a "blinkering effect on perception." Humans necessarily "see with a theory-informed gaze," and "a wrong theory distorts every fact, just as the truth rightly interprets every fact."[129] But one gets the clear sense that the type of "theory" Powlison usually has in mind is *ultimate-level* theory. We see this when he compares "false theories" with

---

128. If, using again Marsden's terminology, Myers is a Warfieldian vis-à-vis apologetics, Roberts might be a Kuyperian. See Marsden, *Understanding Fundamentalism and Evangelicalism*, ch. 5. The genius of Van Til's apologetic—represented by Powlison—is that it reconciles the Warfieldian emphasis on rational proof and evidence with the Kuyperian emphasis on antithetical worldviews.

129. Powlison, "Biblical Counseling View," 201.

"the Faith" and says that "information and observation must always be subjected to analysis from the standpoint of the Faith."[130] "Theory and worldview provide the intellectual center of the psychological enterprise, the 'doctrinal core.'"[131] This ultimate-level understanding of theory is also evident when he discusses the lack of a theory able to unify the field of psychology.[132] He is absolutely right when he says, "we often forget something very important. The Faith is a theory whose view of human nature competes head-on with the personality theories."[133] Yet the "personality theories" that he has in mind are the more ultimate-level and "grand" classical theories, such as those of Adler and Freud, which are dismissed by mainstream psychology today as unscientific. Still, Powlison is correct to think of our faith as a "theistic rational system" that "is directly opposed by naturalistic rational systems,"[134] though perhaps today we might prefer to conceptualize our faith more as a story. He is also certainly right to claim that theory—when conceived in this ultimate sense—is institutionalized: "Power is wielded because theories and therapies are institutionalized."[135] Theories in Powlison's mind address big questions: there is a "big WHY? that anchors every theory."[136] When he talks about how psychology lacks a "bridging theory"[137] to unify the discipline, he is also referring to an ultimate-level theory, a "Grand Unified Theory."[138] He also speaks this way when he qualifies Kuhn's statement that psychology has no paradigm.[139] It *is* unified in its belief that Christianity is at best irrelevant, Powlison argues.

---

130. Ibid., 202.
131. Ibid., 204–5.
132. Ibid., 206–7.
133. Ibid., 209.
134. Ibid.
135. Ibid., 215.
136. Ibid., 220. But micro-theories are probably more anchored by the empirical realities they attempt to explain.
137. Ibid., 206.
138. Ibid., 207.
139. Ibid., 208.

Here again, Powlison conceptualizes theory as an ultimate-level belief that guides research.

Though Roberts has quite a bit less to say explicitly than Powlison on this matter, the theoretical bent of Roberts is also fairly easy to discern. The Christian psychologies contained in the writings of Augustine and Edwards, for example, or in the Bible itself, were not by and large "micro-theories" dealing with technical and highly-specific aspects of psychological functioning. They were "big picture" ultimate-level theories.

Powlison and Roberts are right. The Christian faith, contrary to what a modern perspectivalist would claim, can function as an ultimate-level theoretical perspective relevant to the interpretation of (and construction of) psychological data.[140] But the Christian faith does not imply that the micro-theories that are the lifeblood of psychological science need to be rejected or even revised. Would "the Faith" endorse Festinger's mere inconsistency approach, Aronson's self-concept, or Cooper's "new look?" The Faith could easily endorse any of these micro-theories. This contest between micro-theories is a battle that needs to be fought in the context of the psychological laboratory. But the Faith does offer the higher-level explanation that renders dissonance phenomena (and each of the prevailing micro-theories) ultimately intelligible in a way that naturalism/Darwinism does not.

"Integration" as a Failed Alternative?
On the surface of things, one might think that the "integration" approach discussed by Gary Collins would provide a framework to marry the good of these two perspectivalist approaches. If modern perspectivalism emphasizes the book of God's works, and postmodern perspectivalism emphasizes the book of God's words, integration advocates have long argued that the two books of God's revelation ought to be read together. To this end,

---

140. In my own "Reformational" philosophical tradition, it is more customary to conceive of the Christian faith as "pre-theoretical" rather than theoretical, and I would agree that it is indeed pre-theoretical. But worldview beliefs can be (and often are) made explicit in scientific discussions. They then become part of the network of theoretical beliefs.

Collins approvingly quotes psychologists Paul Meehl who said that he took "it for granted that revelation [i.e., Scripture] cannot genuinely *contradict* any truth about man or the world which is discoverable by other means,"[141] and Harold Faw who believes that since "God has revealed himself in both his world and his Word, one's grasp of his truth, finite and faltering though it is, will be enhanced by bringing these sources of truth together."[142]

Also, just as modern perspectivalism emphasizes common grace and postmodern perspectivalism antithesis, integration thinkers have espoused something similar to the balanced approach that I advocate. Clearly, the very fact that integrationists desire to bring theology and psychology together implies that psychology has something worthwhile to offer. It is just as clear that Collins writes with a clear sense of how Christianity is suppressed by the mainstream, recounting how during his graduate school days, "my professors largely ignored religion, and whenever it was mentioned in our textbooks the references were always negative,"[143] so that he would during his training have "to pretend that God did not exist in the counseling room."[144] He says that psychology still clings "tenaciously to a rapidly disappearing, Enlightenment-based logical positivism."[145]

Despite these promising signs, and despite the fact that during the 1970s and 80s Collins inspired many psychologists with an "extraordinary integration vision,"[146] Collins's essay in 2000 seemed to indicate that the integration movement was in bad shape. Collins very honestly admitted that although "academic institutions have promised prospective students that integration is at the core of their educational programs,"[147] "we still don't agree on what the word *integration* means,"[148] that "the term

---

141. Collins, "Integration View," 103.
142. Ibid., 109.
143. Ibid., 102.
144. Ibid., 119.
145. Ibid., 109.
146. Jones, "Integration View," 104.
147. Collins, "Integration View," 103–4.
148. Ibid., 104.

remains confusing,"[149] and that *Integration* has become a word shrouded in mystery, a slogan, a buzzword that gives us warm feelings but is used more as a gimmick to attract students than as a genuine scholarly achievement or a practical methodology."[150]

Though this was perhaps not his main goal, Collins's essay emphasizes the confusion that can exist among integrationists— "there is no agreement about what we are integrating," indeed, "integration is undefinable."[151] The targets of integration move—theology changes, psychology changes, clinical practice changes. Plus, approaches to integration are deeply personal— "surely there is a Gary Collins approach to counseling, writing, and teaching," but this is only one person's approach and it would be arrogant to lay it down as "*the* biblical approach."[152] Plus there are a multitude of considerations that integrationists need to incorporate, such as a deeper understanding of hermeneutics, eschatological orientation, cultural sensitivity, the question of outreach—how clinicians and academics need to dialogue and how to engage in social action.

In short, Collins's chapter attempts to "integrate" too much and seems, in the end, to have to make some difficult concessions. For example, at the end of the essay Collins says, "I wish I could give a formula for integration,"[153] but he cannot. There are no "rules for integrating faith with practice."[154] At times, he seems to question the entire project, fearing that "we have systematized and intellectually conceptualized psychology and theology so much that we have squeezed out the spiritual."[155] Instead, he says, we must rely on the Holy Spirit so that "our lives become walking examples of integration."

Collins is of course right, that we must rely on the Holy Spirit, and that the way we live our lives is infinitely more important than how airtight our theoretical systems may be.

149. Ibid., 105.
150. Ibid., 105.
151. Ibid., 112.
152. Ibid., 115.
153. Ibid., 125.
154. Ibid., 126.
155. Ibid.

(This is why I also feel that what the biblical counseling approach has to offer is ultimately of much greater value than what I have to offer.) Yet, theoretical life, for all of its limitations, is still a part of life, particularly for those called to academic vocations as teachers or students—we must learn to think well. And part of thinking well, as any teacher who has provided guidance on a term paper can attest, requires that we narrow our focus of attention. We need to ask, "Whose psychology? Which Christianity?" In my calling, I am interested in the relationship between my confessional Reformed Christianity and the psychological science that I teach my students day after day. Thus defined, my "integration" problem is not that difficult. (This does not, of course, mean that *solving* the problem is easy.) Any future efforts at integration will likewise need to be more focused in order to be successful.[156]

A Third Perspectivalism—Reformed and Reformational

In what follows I will sketch out the perspective that I have employed in my teaching of psychological science at the university level—a perspective that has emerged as I have read and discussed *Psychology & Christianity: Four Views* with my students over the years.

Antithetical Openheartedness
Any Christian teaching psychological science would need to assume a science-affirming stance, such as that of David Myers. To some extent I live in that same world, read the same articles, use the same textbooks (though he actually *wrote* the textbooks), and teach some of the same courses. I, too, have supervised hundreds of undergraduate students in the design of experimental research projects. As scientific knowledge is public (i.e., replicable) knowledge it is also God's knowledge. Common grace

---

156. The need to be careful in defining terms is certainly not an original idea, but is quite basic in the integration literature. See, for example, Stevenson, Eck, and Hill, *Psychology and Christianity Integration*, 177. This of course once again raises the question of the representativeness of this chapter.

isn't "scattered" here and there in psychological science. If we have eyes to see, it is to be found in every well-designed and valid empirical study.[157] Though often "trivial"[158] from the perspective of ministry, the findings of psychological science, when considered as disclosures of God's handiwork, are *far* from trivial—they glorify the God who made them. Hence, the insights of psychological science are to be embraced with openhearted gratitude and wonder. And for those of us who work in the field, we have no choice but to embrace the good of the discipline.

I also want to maintain the same antithesis-affirming stance as Powlison and Roberts (and Collins). There really are institutional, epistemological, and metaphysical arrangements that exclude the Christian worldview. When considered from a sociological standpoint, psychology has a worldview and it isn't Christian—it is empiricist, and naturalistic.[159] Christians are certainly welcome to work in the discipline, but they are not allowed to challenge psychology's worldview commitments.[160] Interestingly, psychological science increasingly allows for ultimate-level (i.e., Darwinian) explanations of empirical data. We can put a Christian spin on this and say that God directed evolution, but this misses the point. The mainstream believes that Darwinian evolution is in direct opposition to theism, as Pinker and Bloom

---

157. Assuming there has not been a Type I error, that is. There is always a small chance (usually 5 percent in psychology) that incorrect hypotheses will be supported by the data. But over time, these errors can be weeded out when they fail to be replicated.

158. "The more distinctively 'scientific' a bit of psychological knowledge is, the less 'important' it will be" (Powlison, "Biblical Counseling View," 200).

159. In reality the situation is a bit more subtle than this. There is a sense in which any true statement already presupposes the truth of Christianity, but this is not the place to discuss this nuance. For an elaboration of this idea, see Bahnsen, *Van Til's Apologetic*, ch. 6. One upshot of this idea, however, is that true scientific statements are indeed "theory-laden," i.e., they presuppose Christianity! This is why Christians can and should accord the greatest respect to scientific discovery.

160. A recent survey of attitudes toward religion within science finds that many scientists are indeed religious, though scientists tend to feel they must keep their faith "closeted" (Ecklund, *Science vs. Religion*, 43–45).

attest.[161] Plus, even those Christians who assume that God directed human evolution (a non-Darwinian position, I may add) cannot be content with the incessant interpretive move of psychological science to reduce everything to adaptation for survival and reproduction (which presupposes a Darwinian rather than a distinctively Christian view of evolution).

Bridging Ultimate- and Proximate-level Psychological Theorizing
Psychology is simply one of many academic disciplines that has in its recent history been shaped by an "evolution revolution" in which "the metanarrative of Darwinian thought" is being applied to "make sense" of vast stretches of human culture and experience. "For better or for worse, we live in the Age of Biology." Ironically, from the vantage point of Christian faith, this can be for the better. Though the Darwinian story has had a powerful impact on psychological science since its inception as an independent scientific discipline, never before has its function as an ultimate-level metanarrative been clearer.

The implication would seem to be this—since ultimate-level worldview beliefs do currently and powerfully shape theoretical activity in psychological science, Christians ought to insist that their own ultimate-level worldview beliefs be allowed to compete in the interpretive game of psychological science. This can, of course, be done well or done poorly. Nevertheless, attempts to demonstrate the coherence between ultimate-level (theological and philosophical) and proximate-level (meta- and micro-theoretical) beliefs ought to play at least some role in a distinctively Christian engagement with psychology. Certainly the biblical counseling and Christian Psychology approaches would have much to contribute to the articulation of these ultimate-level beliefs.

As a brief and superficial example, in the realm of dissonance theory, the Christian worldview would not presumably dictate under which circumstances any of the current micro-theories would hold (this would be a strictly empirical question), although it could provide an ultimate-level accounting for them

---

161. Bloom, *How Pleasure Works*, 4; Pinker, *Language Instinct*, 352.

all (consistent with Festinger's notion of mere consistency, human beings as the *imago dei* would presumably desire to be consistent with themselves, for example). Further, the meta-theoretical idea that humans have a need to see themselves (i.e., not merely be seen by others) in a positive moral light would also cohere nicely with a Christian anthropology. Again, such an accounting would not strictly speaking be "scientific" in the traditional proximate-level sense. It would be scientific only in the sense that Darwinian stories are scientific—i.e., that it provides a meta-narrative that coheres with what has been observed. The superiority of the Christian meta-narrative vis-à-vis Darwinism will be addressed below.

Non-reductive, Trans-aspectual Theorizing
An adequate approach to psychological science will concern itself with the multi-aspectual interrelatedness of human psychological functioning, without reducing this functioning to any single aspect. As we have seen, the Biblical cCounseling and Christian Psychology approaches not only tend to emphasize ultimate-level (more integrative) theorizing, but they also tend to focus in this theorizing on the life of faith and morality, the so-called "pistic" and ethical aspects of functioning, while a levels-of-explanation approach, with its implicit preference for micro-theories, tends to focus on the more mundane topics that characterize the discipline as it currently exists. The non-reductive, trans-aspectual approach that I am advocating would retain the insight of Powlison and Roberts that properly-directed pistic and ethical functioning is crucial to human flourishing, but it would also take counsel from the multitudinous other areas of psychological science and their contribution to our understanding of human functioning.

A Symmetrical, Hermeneutical, and Doxological Approach
With this full-orbed view of theory in place, Christians in psychology can (and must) keep both books open. The scientific methods employed in psychology should be understood as sophisticated but limited ways of reading the book of God's works. We can whole-heartedly encourage psychological science

to continue to develop these methods. But by insisting that the data- and micro-theory-levels of psychology are not hermetically sealed from worldview considerations, we can then insist that the book of God's Word provides the only ultimate-level perspective that renders the facts of experience intelligible. As Collins notes, there is a hermeneutical side to reading both books, and we should never expect to have a final read on either text. We should also always be working on improving our read of *both* texts—and reading both texts needs to be part of our *psychological* work. But as a Reformed Christian and a teacher of psychological science, I am convinced that accurate and insightful interpretations of both texts are readily available, and that the harmony that already exists between the two books is remarkable. Our job is to show that this is the case. I have argued that we ought to intentionally seek as the end of our psychological work God's own ultimate end in making the world—the glory of his own name. Demonstrating the harmony of the two books is one way Christians in psychology can fulfill this goal.

Engaged Presuppositionalism
Like Myers, then, I want to affirm that psychological science does not by and large contradict Christian commitment. He has laid down an admirable path of evidential apologetic engagement (flowing out of his detailed knowledge of psychological science) and has garnered the respect of the world's leaders in psychological science. But like Powlison, coming from the same Van Tillian vantage point, I want to say something bolder than "Christians are rational," or, perhaps, "Christians aren't crazy for being Christian." Instead, we want to argue that the Christian worldview is actually true, and therefore provides an ultimate-level explanation superior to the biological reductionism of Darwinism. But Biblical Counseling, as a pastoral movement within the church, has not brought the light of God's Word into the academic discipline of psychology itself. Psychological science, when considered from the vantage point of such pastoral con-

cern, may seem fairly trivial or unimportant,[162] and pastors may not have time to read psychological science. However, Christians in psychological science need to apply Powlison's bold statements about the explanatory superiority of "the Faith" to their own areas of expertise. This would almost certainly need to be a collaborative effort among diversely skilled individuals all committed to a sweeping and unifying Christian vision for psychological science. When we *show, in hundreds of specific ways, that indeed* the Faith does better, we will have constructed "one long argument"[163] not only for the truth of Christianity, but also for the necessity of explicitly Christian perspective within psychological science.

For the last seven years or so I have been calling this apologetic approach *transcendental* perspectivalism. The word "transcendental" indicates that the approach is a type of argument, an argument that asks about the preconditions of experience. Made famous by Immanuel Kant in arguing that proximate-level categories such as cause and effect and the self are necessary in order to render experience intelligible, this type of argument was developed into a full-fledged apologetic by Cornelius Van Til when he shifted the question to one of worldview—which *worldview* is actually presupposed in experience?[164] His two-step argument, again, is to first, for the sake of argument, put the lens of your unbelieving interlocutor on and ask if things cohere,

---

162. This is unfortunate—there is much in psychological science that can help Christians.

163. This famous phrase comes from the opening line in the final chapter of Darwin, *Origin of Species*.

164. For an elaboration of this understanding of Van Til, see Bahnsen, *Van Til's Apologetic*. There are many within the Reformational philosophical camp who think Van Til's approach is "transcendent" rather than transcendental. and to some extent I think that is an accurate point—the Christian worldview can serve as an "Archimedian point" from which we can view all of reality, which, as Dooyeweerd said, is a transcendent vantage point. Still, I think we can frame Van Til's argument as transcendental by showing how Van Til is concerned with ultimate-level preconditions of knowledge (i.e., the ontological Trinity), while Dooyeweerd—like Kant—was concerned with certain proximate-level preconditions (i.e., for Dooyeweerd, the inner nature and structure of theoretical thought per se). But this is not the place to develop this argument.

make sense, and come into focus when wearing these lenses. This is not hard to do because psychological science is *already* engaged in a form of *Darwinian* transcendental perspectivalism, attempting to show how the Darwinian worldview is presupposed in and therefore makes ultimate sense of the facts of psychological science. (And in their attempts to do this we find the best examples of the limits of that paradigm).

The second step of the argument is to ask our unbelieving interlocutors to put on the lens of the Christian worldview and ask the same question, "Do these findings or successful microtheories come into focus/make sense/cohere when looked at from the vantage point of the Christian worldview?" Van Til's disarmingly strong assertion years ago that every fact makes sense only in view of the Christian worldview has in my own experience fit the findings of psychological science very well. We may begin, as Van Til did, with the assumptions of science itself (the lawfulness of the world and the reliability of reason)—these make much more sense in a Christian theistic context than in a naturalistic/Darwinist one.

Then we move on to the findings of psychological science themselves: the mysterious complexity of sense perception that goes well beyond the complexity of individual sense organs such as the eye; the fact that the left hemisphere has an "interpreter module" that seeks to construct plausible stories; that the human brain is, as evolutionary psychologist Geoffrey Miller put it, "wildly in excess of what . . . we would need to survive";[165] that human beings can discriminate about one million different colors, that human beings create music and experience emotions like awe; that humans have the innate capacity to learn syntax-

---

165. Buckner and Whittlessey, "Why Sex?" The full quote, which I love: "The human brain is the most complex system in the known universe. It's wildly in excess of what it seems like we would need to survive on the plains of Africa. In fact, the human brain seems so excessive that a lot of people who believe in evolution—applied to plants and animals—have real trouble imagining how natural selection produced the human brain . . . I think people are perfectly sensible in being skeptical about the ability of selection for survival to account for the human brain." Again, Miller argues that it is Darwin's theory of *sexual* selection that can do the heavy theoretical lifting (see footnote 56).

structured language; that human beings seem to have a deep need to justify themselves, etc. Each of these phenomena is difficult—sometimes exceedingly difficult—to account for in terms of gradualist Darwinist predictions, yet each coheres perfectly well with the Christian story. This isn't evidentialist apologetics, where we simply ask our debate partners to follow the data "where they lead"—people don't work that way. If we start in autonomy, we will end in autonomy. But it is an *engaged* presuppositional apologetics—in which we invite our partners to consider another vantage point, to see how well it coheres with the facts of psychology (and there can be no honest doubting that human language, human storytelling, love of music, and physiological complexity cohere with the Christian worldview), and, as Powlison put it, to invite them to intelligent repentance.

In short, transcendental perspectivalism is a fancy name that amounts to a simple yet bold idea—that apart from the Christian worldview psychological science can make ultimate sense neither of itself nor of its findings. Put differently, transcendental perspectivalism is a kind of Reformed/presuppositional natural theology.[166] All facts reveal and presuppose the God of the Christian Scriptures, and are ultimately unintelligible apart from him. The Christian psychologist is called to show that this is indeed the case.[167]

---

166. The problem with traditional natural theology is its assumption of autonomy vis-à-vis nature, as Reformed thinkers have long noted. A presuppositional natural theology affirms what the Reformed tradition has always affirmed and what this essay has argued, that the natural world reveals God. We (i.e., *sinners*) need, however, as Calvin said, the "spectacles of Scripture" in order to *see* that this is the case. For a similar approach, see McGrath, *Open Secret*; McGrath, *Fine-tuned Universe*. Though I have just recently begun studying McGrath's approach, we do seem to share some of the same fundamental ideas, such as the idea that a presupposed (rather than rationally demonstrated) Christian faith, as he puts it, "makes sense" of the facts of science. For a classic statement on a Reformed/presuppositional approach to natural theology, see Van Til, "Nature and Scripture."

167. See Figure C for a summary of the vision for psychological theory described above. Though this is not the place to develop the thought, this approach would provide an ideal context for a revival of old-style, narratively

KOSITS *Whose Psychology? Which Christianity?* 157

Figure C: The structure of theory in psychological science advocated in this essay, using cognitive dissonance theory as an example.

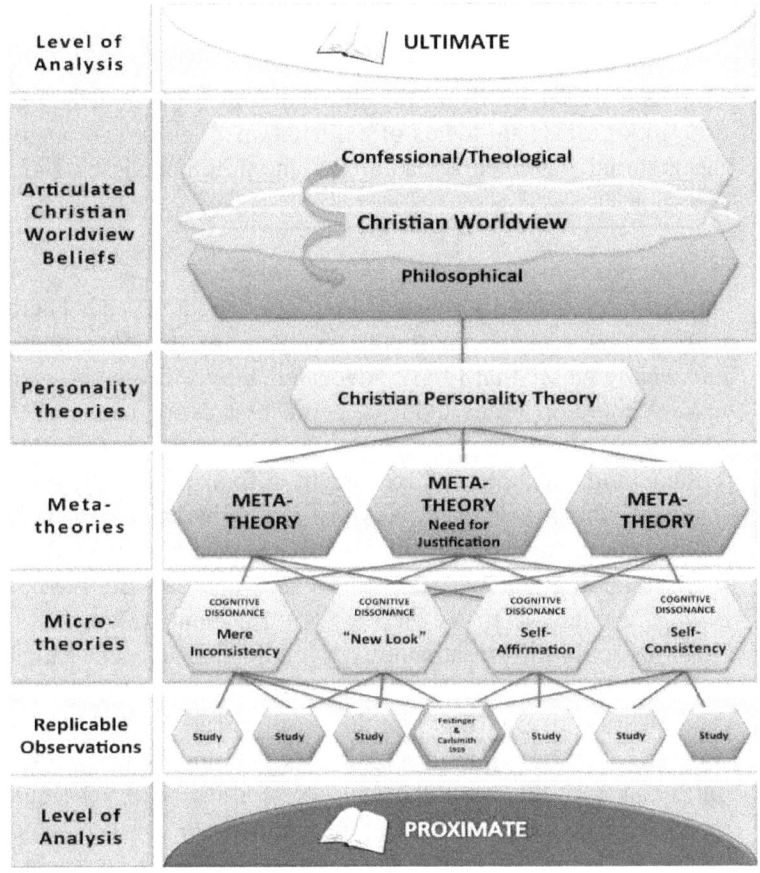

The Second Edition of Psychology & Christianity

Since I have been interacting with the first edition of *Psychology & Christianity* for about seven years, and since my own views have been so powerfully shaped by the first edition, my strategy

---

rich, interdisciplinary personality theories, such as those advocated by Baumeister and Tice, "Rethinking."

in this essay has been to articulate my own position vis-à-vis the first edition before reading the second. In what follows, I will sketch out my initial impressions of the second edition in light of my reading of the first.

Levels-of-Explanation Approach Unchanged
The essay of David Myers is improved in that it contains a better description of what "levels of explanation" means, and some of the material has been updated. But the argument is essentially the same.

A More Winsome Essay on Biblical Counseling
Powlison's beautifully revised essay is a delight to read. There is a clear movement in this essay toward the "antithetical openheartedness" that I have advocated above. The ambivalence toward common grace evident in the first essay seems all but gone, yet with no significant loss of antithesis. The repeated Van Tillian (and, he notes, Augustinian) refrain of how the Faith interprets things rightly strikes just the right balance. The following quote summarizes the tone of the entire essay: "There's work to do and much to learn from many sources. But the credo orients, teaching us to see facts in their true context."[168]

In particular, the treatment of psychological science (which is part of "Psych-2" in his parlance) sounds much less postmodern—he affirms the usefulness of scientific insights, and, dropping the extended discussion of the theory-ladenness of data, correctly identifies the key shortcoming of psychological science: "psychologists tend to be unaware of the problematic nature of their underlying assumptions . . ."[169]

The essay now includes some richly nuanced case study material, belying any who would dismiss biblical counseling as necessarily unsophisticated and simplistic. Powlison also does a wonderful job of conveying how difficult it is to capture concisely the dynamics of God- and Word-centered healing. A

---

168. Powlison, "Biblical Counseling View," in *Five Views*, 248.
169. Ibid., 255.

respectful reader's only choice is to dig deeper before she can draw a final conclusion.

My only criticism of Powlison's essay is that Biblical Counseling as therein construed still seems to leave the light of the CCEF's seminal achievement hidden under the bushel of a strictly church-centric vision. In this vision, the insights of secular psychology are to be mined for the good of the church. But the vision for how the insights of the faith are to be brought to the secular world of counseling seems vague at best. Powlison rightly says that a church with a flourishing counseling ministry will be an attractive missional fragrance in the culture at large. But what I would like to see is a more explicit apologetic agenda for showing the world of secular counseling that the Faith really does do better. This would seem to fulfill the first half of the CCEF's mission statement, "to restore Christ to counseling."

Part of this change would mean that biblical counselors will need to do a better job of acknowledging in very specific ways their deep connections—and, indeed, indebtedness—to secular psychotherapy (implicitly and explicitly evident in Powlison's new essay in many ways). As a ministry for Christians, the CCEF has in its writings emphasized how their approach *differs from* and *improves upon* secular psychotherapy while de-emphasizing what and how much has actually been learned from secular psychology. A better acknowledgment of secular psychology may gain them a greater hearing from the secular world of counseling. As they move in this direction I would see the CCEF doing for the clinical side of the discipline what the agenda described in this essay hopes to do for the scientific side. Further, demonstrating that Christian faith unifies these two perennially estranged and heretofore tenuously connected psychologies would be a powerful apologetic indeed!

A Christian Psychology Collaboration
The "Christian Psychology View" article has also undergone a substantial revision, mostly due to the fact that Robert Roberts has brought along a co-author—a psychological scientist named P. J. Watson, who has done excellent work in a variety of research areas, such as the psychology of religion. Watson has

become one of the leading spokesmen of the Christian Psychology movement, and his thought-provoking 2010 Bryan Institute Symposium presentation—part of the symposium launching the second edition of *Psychology & Christianity*—provided something of an inspiration for the title of this article.[170]

The first half of this new essay now portrays the major idea of the original essay as "step one" in a two-step process. This first step, then, is to retrieve the Christian psychology of the past, and they continue to use Roberts's interesting exegesis of the Sermon on the Mount. One difference in this first section of the essay, however, is that the tone feels more anti-scientific than the original essay.

That tone is corrected in the second half of the essay, written (presumably) by Watson. The second step of Christian Psychology is "operationalizing the Christian tradition," i.e., formulating testable hypotheses of immediate and obvious Christian interest—topics in the psychology of religion primarily. For example, Jesus' Sermon on the Mount explains that "hatred of God is explained by being mastered by Mammon." This explanation could be tested empirically. He cites other studies, such as those that demonstrate a link between prayer and well-being in Christians.

Though these developments are certainly interesting, important, and exciting, this understanding of "the distinctively Chris-

---

[170]. An audio recording of this conference is available online. Watson's session, "Whose Psychology? Which Rationality? Christian Psychology after Postmodernism" can be found at http://www.bryan.edu/9414.html. The talk has also recently appeared in print. My first response to his argument, which admirably attempts to cast "Christian Psychology" as ecumenical and broad in inclusion, was to think that a greater degree of theological specificity would be necessary than he seemed to indicate. After recently re-listening (and then reading the published article), I was pleased to discover deep compatibilities between our approaches. Still, I don't think we can "out-narrate all other positions" without theological particularity. Indeed, my contention is that the Reformed and Reformational position I have laid out in this article provides the kind of narration that Watson calls for. See Watson, "Whose Psychology? Which Rationality? Christian Psychology within an Ideological Surround after Postmodernism," 308.

tian goals of Christian psychology"[171] betrays, I think, too narrow a view of Christianity. This is my Father's world, and it includes more than the faith-related and ethical aspects of life (though, again, these aspects are absolutely central to human flourishing). God created all things, including the brain, sensory processes, human cognition, and language—so these things would seem to cry out for a distinctively Christian understanding as well.

One of Watson's greatest contributions is that he puts flesh on the bones of the well-worn notion that all data are theory-laden. He has for decades been doing careful empirical work within the field of the psychology of religion, demonstrating that worldview bias is built into some of the widely used measures. For example, one scale takes endorsement of the statement, "people need a source of strength outside themselves";[172] as evidence of irrational belief. Another scale characterizes the belief, "God exists" as an indication of "existential avoidance."[173] By subjecting scales to careful conceptual and empirical scrutiny and revising some of the measures, Watson shows that they become much more useful when studying Christian populations. Christians in psychological science should pay careful attention to Watson's techniques for detecting when worldview bias has been built into the supposedly scientific measures themselves.

But the field of the psychology of religion has always been on the periphery of mainstream psychological science, and researchers within that domain have been perceived by the mainstream as being biased (either pro-religion or anti-religion).[174] Watson's helpful work shows very clearly that this is the case! But there are many areas of psychology where the measures are not often in any obvious way anti-Christian. In Festinger and Carlsmith's seminal cognitive dissonance study, described in detail above, participants were asked:

---

171. Roberts and Watson, "Christian Psychology View," 166.
172. Ibid., 172.
173. Ibid., 168.
174. Baumeister, "Religion and Psychology," 165.

> Were the tasks interesting and enjoyable? In what way? In what way were they not? Would you rate how you feel about them on a scale from -5 to +5 where -5 means they were extremely dull and boring, +5 means they were extremely interesting and enjoyable, and zero means they were neutral, neither interesting nor uninteresting.[175]

As is the case in many areas of psychological science, there are no obvious anti-Christian worldview assumptions contained in these questions. Indeed, Watson concedes the point, saying that there are many topics being investigated in psychology "that are not as worldview dependent,"[176] such as neuro-psychology, schizophrenia, and social influence. This quote, which comes at the end of the essay, seems to be a significant and problematic concession, for a variety of reasons. First, one could argue that most of the major research areas in the academic discipline psychology would fall into this category—neuropsychology, sensation and perception, language, cognition and memory, affective science, social psychology—most of the chapters in an introductory psychology textbook. Are we to think that Christian perspectives are unimportant in these areas? If so, this "Christian Psychology View" applies only to a narrow slice of psychological science and stands in essential agreement with a levels-of-explanation approach for the rest. Hence, the Christian Psychology approach appears to concede too much space to "the establishment." Perhaps this concession is made because those areas that can be investigated empirically are "less 'interesting'"[177] than the areas where conflict is obvious. But the bigger issue is Watson's focus on the proximate-level aspect of psychological science—if anti-Christian worldview assumptions are embedded in the measures themselves, then we need to reassess. But, as I have been arguing, the most important way—though certainly not the only way—that anti-Christian worldview assumptions in mainstream psychological science manifest

---

175. Festinger and Carlsmith, "Cognitive Consequences," 206.
176. Roberts and Watson, "Christian Psychology View," 173.
177. Ibid., 154.

themselves is in the realm of ultimate-level interpretations of data.

With these considerations in mind, I would like to propose a third step in the Christian Psychology agenda. I fully endorse the first step—retrieving the Christian psychology of the past. Indeed, in my history of psychology class we read Jonathan Edwards's *Religious Affections* and follow Roberts's guidelines for discerning the Christian psychology contained therein. I fully endorse the second step—individual measures need to be scrutinized according to Christian presuppositions, and topics of distinctive Christian interest ought to be pursued empirically. But Christian Psychology needs a third step that encourages Christians to enter into the thick waters of interpretation of mainstream psychological science. We need to look carefully at the current state of psychological science—those domains of psychology that are not in any obvious way, as Watson says, "worldview dependent," nevertheless filter these hard-won proximate-level findings through the lens of an increasingly explicit and aggressively totalizing ultimate-level evolutionary worldview. Introductory psychology students are exposed to "the unshakable foundations of Darwinian theory,"[178] and are told that "the idea that the machinery of behavior and mind evolved through natural selection" is one of the "three foundation ideas for psychology."[179] Again, this is not to enter into the "creation vs. evolution" debate, which only distracts us from the main issue—the current sociology of psychological science now routinely gives ultimate-level explanatory status to that which is not ultimate. An engaged Christian psychology approach will attempt to enter this discussion head-on and show that Christian assumptions do better in making ultimate-level sense of psychology's proximate-level scientific findings.

---

178. Gerrig et al., *Psychology and Life*, 68. The idea being conveyed in this section of the text is that Darwinian theory is sound because it now sits securely on the "unshakable foundations" of Mendelian genetics.

179. Gray, *Psychology*, 8, 2.

Integration Presented as a Viable Option

Certainly P. J. Watson's contribution has strengthened the second edition of *Psychology & Christianity*. But perhaps the greatest improvement in the second edition of the textbook is the revision to the chapter on "the integration view." The chapter is written by Stanton Jones, a psychology professor at Wheaton College, one of the leading centers for the integration of psychology and Christianity. I am grateful that Jones pays homage to Gary Collins, the author of the original chapter on the integration view, as having inspired him to pursue a career in integration through the "extraordinary integration vision" that Collins had articulated in the late 1970s. Whereas the original chapter unintentionally portrayed integration as a being in a state of confusion, the new chapter has restored the luster of Collins's original, extraordinary vision.

Jones does exactly what needs to be done when one is in the business of relating faith to science—he defines his terms. Though Jones defines psychology as both science and practice, he thankfully emphasizes "the scientific aspects"[180] of psychology in this essay—which makes the essay immediately more relevant to folks like me charged with teaching psychological science, while not losing its usefulness for practitioners.

Jones certainly advocates something akin to a two-books approach, giving Scripture its primary epistemological place.[181] Indeed, his definition of integration makes the issue primary:

> *Integration of Christianity and psychology (or any area of "secular thought") is our living out—in this particular area—of the lordship of Christ over all existence by our giving his special revelation— God's true Word—its appropriate place of authority in determining*

---

180. Jones, "Integration View," 105.
181. Though Jones may not intend to do so, one potential problem with his formulation is that he seems to portray God's actions and God's words as having to do with a limited aspect of creation, while other parts of creation, such as neurons and memory, fall outside of God's actions and words. I will elaborate on this in the conclusion.

our fundamental beliefs about and practices toward all of reality and toward our academic subject matter in particular.[182]

However, because Scripture "does not provide us all that we need in order to understand human beings fully,"[183] the careful study of creation is also warranted. He recalls how Collins had "called for Christians to draw on all the riches of Scripture"[184] in their integrative efforts. In his example of empirical research in the area of homosexuality, Jones demonstrates careful and respectful attention to the scriptural data relevant to that particular question. By focusing on the scientific evidence, he likewise gives emphasis to a careful reading of the book of God's Works.

There is likewise a clear affirmation of common grace and antithesis in Jones's essay, though not formulated in that language. For example, he speaks often of the areas of "tension" that exist between Christianity and psychological science. He rightly notes that "it is common today to view science in such a way that religious faith of any kind can have no impact on science or interaction with science,"[185] such as Gould's position that science and faith can coexist so long as we assume that God has nothing to do with empirical happenings. And, very clearly, as a psychological scientist, Jones is highly receptive to empirical work.

Jones likewise does not explicitly address the multi-aspectual nature of human functioning, but his approach would seem to embrace the concerns addressed in this essay. As a psychological scientist, Jones finds interesting all aspects of human functioning, not just the traditionally religious or ethical. He also appears to share an aversion to reductive theories, explaining that the reductionism of the personality theories he encountered as a student was one of the early catalysts driving him toward an integrationist position.

---

182. Jones, "Integration View," 102.
183. Ibid., 101.
184. Ibid., 104.
185. Ibid., 105.

There does not seem to be much of an apologetic edge in Jones's essay. He seems more concerned with faithfully working through areas of "tension" between psychology and Christianity, articulating a position consistent with Scripture, rather than showing that the Christian worldview actually clarifies or improves psychology itself.

This neglect is related to his way of construing psychological theory. At times, Jones seems to vacillate between what I have called "modern perspectivalism" and "postmodern perspectivalism" in his essay. In an important section of the essay, Jones discusses "how science really operates,"[186] making the typical postmodern points that data are theory-laden, that theories are underdetermined by facts and that science is always a human endeavor that "must utilize metaphysically and ethically loaded concepts."[187] Though there is much truth to all of this, these ideas neglect the fact that there really are differences between proximate-level micro-theories, and more ultimate-level worldview commitments. Certainly these influence each other, but many micro-theories in psychological science are not fatally corrupted, as I have attempted—at least in a preliminary way—to show.

On the other hand, there are times when Jones (like Roberts and Watson) sounds a bit like a modern perspectivalist, when he concedes that "there are . . . many areas of psychological study where the most basic construals that nonbelieving scientists make about their subject matter are roughly in accord with how Christians might view the same subject."[188] In particular he has in mind areas "to which Scripture does not speak," such as "how neurons work, how the brain synthesizes mathematical or emotional information, the types of memory, or the best way to conceptualize personality traits."[189] But how is it possible, if psychological science is "metaphysically and ethically loaded,"

---

186. Ibid., 113.
187. Ibid., 115.
188. Ibid., 116.
189. Ibid.

that there can be so many areas of psychological science that seem unproblematic?

Again, if we keep in mind the proximate/ultimate distinction, alongside the idea that, on an ultimate level there are *no* areas "to which the Scripture does not speak," we can make some headway here. Though we need to be careful not to oversimplify the distinction, there really is a difference between scientifically rigorous empirical observation and ultimate-level interpretation. Such an approach will help us to avoid dichotomizing psychological science into areas of tension and areas of agreement. Insofar as we are dealing with publically accessible and empirically replicated data, there is agreement.[190] But insofar as we are dealing with the interpretation of these data, we will disagree, even when we are talking about neurons or memory. And since psychological science deals not only with data but also with higher-order interpretation, Christians in psychology must not concede this interpretive space to naturalism.

The New "Transformational" Approach
The textbook's new essay on "the transformational psychology view" is written by John H. Coe and Todd W. Hall, both professors at Biola University, home of the Rosemead School of Psychology (a hub for the integration of psychology and theology), Talbot School of Theology, and the Institute for Spiritual Formation. Coe is Professor of Philosophy and Spiritual Theology, and Director of the Institute of Spiritual Formation. Hall is Professor of Psychology, and Director of the Institute for Research on Psychology and Spirituality. Rosemead offers doctoral degrees in clinical psychology and publishes the *Journal of Psychology and Theology* (edited by Hall, which tends to emphasize the clinical side of the discipline). The Institute for

---

190. We need, of course, to keep Watson's work in mind here—it is possible that replicable anti-Christian operationalizations are in play. Also, this is not to say that trustworthy findings in science will never appear to contradict Scripture. Though such contradictions may eventually lead us to re-interpret the Bible (as Myers suggests), we need to remember that scientific findings often change over time, while the inspired Scriptures never do.

Spiritual Formation publishes the *Journal of Spiritual Formation and Soul Care*, which "serves as an evangelical forum for the theory and practice of Christian Spirituality."[191] Coe edits this journal. Given these emphases at Biola, it is not particularly surprising that Coe and Hall's essay tends to emphasize spirituality, spiritual formation, and the "clinical" or helping side of the discipline. In short, they offer a "spiritual formation model of psychology," which includes the move from "understanding *to* treatment."[192]

It should be noted that this chapter is a distillation of their book *Psychology in the Spirit: Contours of a Transformational Psychology*, which was published by IVP in January 2010, about six months before the second edition of *Psychology & Christianity*. I am open to the possibility that some of the questions raised by their chapter-length treatment may be resolved in what appears to be a long (446-page) and wide-ranging book.

Though couched in theological language that is at times, to me at least, a bit vague, the basic affirmation of the transformational psychology viewpoint is straightforward enough. Their approach articulates a yet-to-be-realized ideal in which psychology and psychologist both are transformed so that they better align with God's purposes. The foundation of a transformational psychology, Coe and Hall emphasize, is the person herself. A person being transformed by the Holy Spirit will be open to reality, they argue, free from pathological and sinful distortion, and thus able to produce a body of literature (focusing on self, sin, and health) that will help in the practice of helping counselees grow as persons, which leads to further transformation of the psychologist herself. Thus, the transformed psychologist is the alpha and the omega of a transformational psychology approach.

Though there is much to affirm in this new chapter, I struggled to find answers to the questions that frame this essay, Whose Psychology? Which Christianity? Given the primacy of the person, Coe and Hall argue that all (Christian and psy-

---

191. Coe, "Call and Task," 2.
192. Coe and Hall, "Transformational Psychology View," 224.

chological) traditions must be considered "secondary"[193] to the truth-seeking psychologist herself. Since "transformation" would seem to presuppose an object or a discipline to transform, this indefiniteness vis-à-vis psychology led me to wonder at times precisely *whose* psychology they are seeking to transform. As one reads the chapter, however, it seems that "psychology" for Coe and Hall is more the domain of spiritual advisors and wise counselors, not primarily the scientific psychology taught in introductory courses in North America.

I also wondered *which Christianity* gave form to this approach. The tradition that seems to drive this vision is that of monastic Christianity, now in vogue in certain Evangelical circles, such as Biola. The posture of monastic retreat helps to understand the approach that the transformational model takes toward the already-existing psychologies. A person desiring to become a transformational psychologist will inevitably be in some sense connected to a tradition, they argue, but, just as a monk will for the sake of enlightenment pull himself out of society, a transformational psychologist will look "behind the veil"[194] of his tradition in order to forward his own quest for "firsthand"[195] spiritual and psychological knowledge.

The transformational approach may be in essential agreement with the two books approach advocated here. In addition to careful reflection on "preexisting psychological/scientific/theological reflections and theories," a transformational psychologist will pay careful attention to "whatever is relevant from (1) Scripture, [and] (2) creation."[196] But the chapter also seems to put strong emphasis on spiritual experience. The "firsthand work" of a transformational psychologist involves openness to "the experience of the Spirit and . . . the truths from Scripture, *as well as* . . . truths from observation and reflection."[197] Though spiritual experience is certainly a crucial datum for any Christian

---

193. Ibid., 201.
194. Ibid.
195. Ibid., 202.
196. Ibid., 207–8.
197. Ibid., 202–3.

psychology, a Reformed and Reformational approach to knowledge would be exceedingly cautious in how such experience is utilized. In the Reformed tradition, the pervasiveness of sin (i.e., total depravity) means that all of our ideas—and experiences—are liable to be self-serving or deceptive and must therefore be tested against Scripture.[198] In the mystical spirituality that seems to permeate the transformational view,[199] such interpretive caution seems less necessary—God speaks directly to the human heart.

The rigorous interpretive caution associated with *sola scriptura* has its analogy in psychological science, of course. As Myers says, whenever possible, we should put testable ideas to the empirical test, checking our cherished notions against the text of the book of God's Works. Indeed, the rigors of the scientific method developed in the scientific revolution may have been inspired by the rigors of Protestant biblical exegesis,[200] and were religiously motivated by a keen sense of how human sin and limitation distorts knowledge.[201] Any "openness to the experience of the Spirit" that lacks analogous rigor would seem, at least on the surface of things, to violate the historical "two books" principle. I don't know for sure how Coe and Hall would treat this matter, so I raise the issue only as a point for further discussion and clarification.

Likewise, there are moments when the transformational approach seems to balance the poles of the Kuyperian paradox, such as when they affirm, though somewhat vaguely, that "the

---

198. The best example I know of this is Jonathan Edwards's *Religious Affections*, which deeply probes the Scriptures to discern what sort of spiritual experiences are authentically Spirit-wrought, and which may not be. Perhaps Coe and Hall would endorse such an approach.

199. For a brief introduction to the Desert Fathers, whom Coe and Hall admire, see González, *Story of Christianity*, 1:138–43. Anthony, one of the great Desert Fathers, was said to wrestle with demons and receive visions from God.

200. For example, during the Reformation, "a return to the sources was urged: to the Book of the Scripture in one case, to the book of nature . . . in the other." (Hooykaas, *Religion and the Rise of Modern Science*, 112.)

201. Harrison, *Fall of Man and the Foundations of Science*.

unbeliever, by common grace, is partially able to apprehend the truth of something."[202] The tenor of the chapter, however, seems to lean toward antithesis. We are told, for example, "the *spiritual-emotional development of the psychologist is foundational* to the process of arriving at deep truths about human nature."[203] Though this statement raises important epistemological questions that I will address below, and though statements such as these are usually qualified to suggest that non-Christians can still learn interesting things, the flavor of the chapter seems fairly negative. The negativity seems especially strong vis-à-vis the scientific side of the discipline. At one point early in the argument, for example, scientific methods themselves seem to be associated with psychologizing "outside of a relationship with God."[204]

The trans-aspectual theorizing that would characterize a Reformed and Reformational approach seems to fall outside of their purview. The strong preference in the transformational approach, as one might expect, appears to be on "pistic" (faith-related) and ethical functioning, i.e., the "spiritual" dimensions of life. On the other hand, it seems that there is likely a role for apologetics in transformational psychology, though they do not say what that role is. The authors explain: "our treatment here of a transformational psychology is not primarily written for the unbeliever; otherwise, much of what follows would require a thoroughgoing apologetic or defense."[205] Given transformational

202. Coe and Hall, "Transformational Psychology View," 214.
203. Ibid., 205.
204. Ibid., 200. Though I trust that this association is inadvertent, it is important to be clear that while the historical ascendency of natural scientific methods in psychology is correlated with secularization, and though such methods are often used to forward philosophical naturalism, we should not assume that these methods imply a naturalistic worldview. Indeed, the usefulness and possibility of such methods does not fit neatly into a naturalistic worldview. As the title of Plantinga's recent book implies, the "conflict" between natural science methods and religion is between science and the religion of naturalism, not between science and theistic religion. See Plantinga, *Where the Conflict Really Lies*. I, of course, want to make claims about Christianity specifically, not "theism" in general.
205. Coe and Hall, "Transformational Psychology View," 204.

psychology's emphasis on Spirit-wrought experience accessible only to Christians, i.e., given the seeming lack of a "point of contact," it would be fascinating to read how they would propose to engage in such an apologetic dialogue.

Psychology, I have argued, ought to bridge ultimate- and proximate-level theorizing, as depicted in Figure C. The transformational approach seems to approach the task differently. Their approach "is less about the relationship between *two distinct fields of methodologies* (science/psychology and theology) . . . and is more about doing *a single unified—though complex—science and psychology of reality.*"[206] This approach is conceptualized as "a single act,"[207] which seems counterintuitive. Given that in psychological theory there are individual empirical studies, micro-theoretical and meta-theoretical levels, in addition to the more ultimate-levels of theorizing, such theorizing does not seem to be one act at all, but a deliberate, laborious, multi-step team effort. Though Coe and Hall are right in seeking to correct "a wrong turn in the history of modern science, which bifurcated the world into the 'scientific' and the 'ethical-religious,'" it does not follow that there is "no [methodological] distinction" between the way we study "natural phenomena" and "the contents of Scripture,"[208] for example. I would like to hear more from them on how they propose to do this in "a single act."

The strong emphasis on the spiritual formation of the psychologist actually connects to transcendental perspectivalism in an interesting way. My approach has been influenced by the "triperspectival" epistemology of John Frame.[209] Frame argues that knowledge always involves a *subject* (his "existential perspective"), an *object* (his "situational" perspective), and a *standard* by which we justify our knowledge claims (his "normative" perspective). Building on this framework, I have sometimes referred

---

206. Ibid., 207.
207. Ibid., 200.
208. Ibid., 206.
209. As described in a variety of his works, including Frame, *Doctrine of the Knowledge of God.*

to my position as transcendental *tri*-perspectivalism, where the transcendental question (what are the necessary preconditions for *x*?) can be applied to the necessary characteristics of the *person* himself, asking, "What kind of person do we need to be in order to psychologize well?"; of the *object*, asking, "What sorts of things do we need to study to psychologize well?"; and of the *norm*, asking, "What sort of epistemological standards are necessary in order to psychologize well?" In this essay I have emphasized the normative side of things, arguing that the worldview afforded by the Scriptures (our ultimate epistemic norm) provides superior ultimate-level interpretation of replicable proximate-level findings.

Although *all* of the perspectives in *Psychology & Christianity* could be re-framed in these tri-perspectival terms, Coe and Hall—despite the questions I have raised—do raise some particularly important points about both the existential and situational perspectives. Existentially, as noted above, they put great emphasis on the spiritual formation of the psychologist herself—this *is* a point that has perhaps been underemphasized. It is the attitudes, experiences, and maturity of "the person doing psychology"[210] that are the keys to transformational psychology. Though they seem to underemphasize the sociological and cultural constraints of "doing psychology," when they say, "the transformation of the psychologist is the determinative and foundational element for the process and product of doing psychology,"[211] they are right that apart from authentic spiritual experience, a psychologist will not have access to at least *some* of the "deep truths about human nature,"[212] and will—from their vantage point in the *civitas terrena*—inevitably psychologize for some motive other than the love and glory of God. Cole and Hall also rightly note that the "realities of faith" are not actually propositions *per se*, but certainties accessible only to those transformed by the Spirit.

---

210. Coe and Hall, "Transformational Psychology View," 201.
211. Ibid., 205–6.
212. Ibid., 205.

This, then, has implications when we look at psychological knowledge from a situational perspective, i.e., from the perspective of the *objects* of knowledge. A Christian psychologist, who has access to these "realities of faith," understands that these realities are psychological phenomena that must be included in a truly comprehensive understanding of mental life. It would follow, if psychology is indeed the study of mental life, that we ought not to exclude these psychological realities from our study even if they are difficult to access with traditional empirical methodologies. "A particular scientific or psychological methodology does not dictate reality."[213] Amen!

These are relevant insights not only for counselors, but also for those of us who teach the scientific side of the discipline. What is lacking, however, is any practical sense of how to implement these insights, particularly for a person like me, charged with teaching psychological science. Coe and Hall ask us to look "behind the veil" of current practice and re-imagine what psychology might look like outside of the context and categories of tradition. This is of course necessary for those of us interested in "redeeming psychology,"[214] and I would heartily concur that we need to "be willing to rigorously and painstakingly observe and reflect on whatever is relevant"[215] to psychology. But how precisely ought these things be brought together in the context of a traditional psychology curriculum? Coe and Hall claim that "the person determines the process" of doing psychology, which in turn "determine[s] the product[s]" of psychology. But for those of us charged with teaching traditional psychology courses, such as introduction to psychology, research methods, social psychology, or cognitive psychology, the process and the products are already to a large extent determined before we teachers even begin to interact with the material.

In other words, whether it intends to or not, the transformational approach raises the crucial question of *cultural* transformation. Coe and Hall rightly claim that—within their

---

213. Ibid., 203.
214. Kosits, "What Would It Mean to Redeem Psychology?"
215. Coe and Hall, "Transformational Psychology View," 207.

own circles at least—psychology itself and the institutions in which it is taught ought to be transformed. But just how can a culture (like psychological science) be changed? This is a question that has received a great deal of attention lately, with books such as Andy Crouch's *Culture Making* and James Davison Hunter's *To Change the World*. And to that question we shall turn, as we conclude this essay.

Conclusion: The Varieties of Christian Commitment and the Culture of Psychological Science

At the beginning of this essay I suggested that the key orienting questions in the psychology-Christianity dialogue are: *Whose Psychology, Which Christianity?* My concern has been the interplay between psychological science and a particular—"Reformed and Reformational"—variety of Christian commitment. My hope is that this essay will provide at least some sense of the potential fecundity of such a commitment for Christians desiring to engage contemporary psychology in an integrally Christian way. I have also suggested that Christian approaches to psychology are always filtered though a reading—modern or postmodern—of our cultural moment.

To close this essay, I would like to return to some of these issues, but this time attempting to discern something of the nature of the Christian commitment of each of our authors, and how each variety interacts with *modernity* in particular.[216] Psychological science is still deeply ensconced within the modern worldview. Our engagement with *this* psychology will therefore radically depend on how we think about modernity. I also hope to show that though I tend to disagree with the various stances toward modernity advocated in this book, the Reformed and Reformational approach that I describe in this essay has assimilated insights from all five "views."

---

216. This approach would seem to approximate the two-criterion strategy advocated by Johnson, where we evaluate the nature of an author's Christian commitment, and their relationship to modernity. See Johnson, "Gaining Understanding," 301–2.

David Myers is a brother in the Reformed tradition, teaching at a sister Reformed institution, and a well-respected and established psychological scientist. His laudable respect for empirical reality reflects the old Reformed idea that creation is a divine book to be studied with utmost care. For a concise critique, however, we may turn to Lesslie Newbigin, a brilliant expositor of modern Western culture,[217] who saw the matter clearly: a levels-of-explanation approach, or one that seeks "a *modus vivendi* between science and religion by representing them as [merely] two different ways of seeing the same reality . . . is, I fear, only a particular manifestation of that [modern] dichotomy between the public world of facts and the private world of values . . . "[218] Myers's vision for relating psychology and Christianity, wonderful in many ways, still reflects a kind of approach too decisively shaped by modernity, one that makes it difficult to mount what Newbigin called "a genuinely missionary encounter between the gospel and . . . modern Western culture,"[219] proclaiming Christ as Lord of every square inch of creation. Christians who advocate a levels-of-explanation approach may very well make important contributions to psychological science (and for this reason they deserve our respect), but are unlikely to challenge the convenient but false modern dichotomies between facts and values, faith and reason, that hamstring integrally Christian engagement with the sciences. Nevertheless, the Reformed and Reformational approach advocated in this essay has been powerfully shaped by Myers's enthusiasm for psychological science, and proximate-level empirical work has an absolutely central role to play. Further, my approach is itself a kind of levels-of-explanation approach, albeit one that does not rigidly compartmentalize ultimate- and proximate-levels.

217. Newbigin's description of modernity, his "profile of a culture," is an apt portrayal of the assumptions of contemporary psychological science. See Newbigin, *Foolishness to the Greeks*, ch. 2.
218. Ibid., 66–67.
219. Ibid., 3.

David Powlison, another dear brother in the Reformed tradition, reflects another form of the Reformed tradition profoundly shaped by modernity. Unlike the more accommodating mainstream version of Reformed Protestantism that we see in Myers, Powlison's Westminster Seminary is a product of the tensions reflected in the fundamentalist-modernist controversy of the early twentieth century, established in response to the liberalization of Princeton Seminary in order to preserve traditional Reformed and Presbyterian orthodoxy. Powlison's strong emphasis on the antithesis is a reflection of this reading of the modern cultural situation—Christians are to set themselves against the world and to develop their own, biblically-derived psychology. The fruit of this effort has been a body of insightful and practical writings on human motivation and Christian living—a body that has not yet made contact with mainstream psychological science. I called this approach—especially the version articulated in the first edition of the book—"postmodern" because it sees through the typical modern claims of theoretical and scientific neutrality and instead seeks to venture off and create a "psychology" of its own. Christians who are trained in biblical counseling will have a deep sense of how Scripture speaks to psychological issues but are also unlikely to learn much from or have much hope for mainstream psychology. Still, in the Reformed and Reformational approach that I have outlined in this essay, the insights of the Biblical Counseling Movement would have an important role to play, particularly in ultimate-level theorizing. Further, the devout and respectful attentiveness to Scripture advocated by the Biblical Counseling Movement is something that Christians in psychology ought to emulate.

In the first chapter of his book *Spiritual Emotions*, Robert Roberts discloses a bit of his location within the body of Christ. Both he and his wife have roots in the Reformed tradition—he grew up in the United Presbyterian Church, his wife in the Christian Reformed Church. Upon taking up his post at Wheaton College in 1984, they found a local Reformed congregation overly didactic, and "being as denominationally promiscuous as most Protestants these days," they tried out an Episcopal church, which they eventually joined. *"Theologically rich texts* abounded" in this new environment. "In the Episcopal experience the engendering of spirituality in the service seems to come primarily *from reading*—from the Bible and the Book of Common Prayer—in the context of sensory dramatization. The apostolic tradition is there in all its glory—*in the books*."[220] Perhaps in some sense, then, we might understand the Christian Psychology movement—or at least Roberts's seminal contribution to it—as deeply Episcopalian/Anglican in its sensibilities. The "step one" emphasis of Christian Psychology on carefully reading and "translating" pre-modern texts seems to link to Roberts's experience in the Episcopalian Church. This deeply historical, tradition-rich approach compensates for a weakness in at least some versions of Reformed Christianity, and thus highlights how the diversities within the body of Christ can lead to our mutual edification in our common pursuit. Still, Roberts's reading of the cultural situation has at times felt a bit postmodern, in a manner similar to Powlison's first essay, which has led to a strong emphasis on developing a distinctively Christian psychology and a rejection of mainstream psychology's self-definition as a scientific discipline.[221] Nevertheless, the work of Christian Psychology would also have an important role to play in a Reformed and Reformational approach to psychological science. For example, the "step one" work of Christian Psychology would, like the work of the Biblical Counseling Movement, provide invaluable help in contributing to ultimate-level psychological (i.e., personality) theory. Further, as described above, I see the Reformed and Reformational approach to psychological science described in this article as a potential "step three" in the Christian Psychology approach.

Stanton Jones's wonderful chapter reflects his evangelical faith. One of the great strengths of this faith is its strong emphasis on the authoritative Scriptures, and a refusal to relegate its truth to a "religious" realm or level of explanation that is to be cordoned off from science. Yet there is nevertheless a kind of cordoning that takes place, which represents perhaps the most

---

220. Roberts, *Spiritual Emotions*, 3, 4, 5; emphases mine.
221. Roberts and Watson, "Christian Psychology View," 149.

typical evangelical Christian response to the deterministic tendencies of modernity, in which divine and free human action are *contrasted* with the regular "mechanistic"/cause-and-effect concerns of scientific inquiry.[222] The reason we should not compartmentalize faith and science, Jones explains, is that God sometimes *intervenes* in this natural course of events. Likewise, he argues in another place, the human agent can freely (in an ultimately uncaused/libertarian sense) intervene (if you will) to overcome those determining factors that might otherwise push or pull a human being into sin.[223] Though this avoids the dualism of a *rigid* levels-of-explanation approach in which matters of faith and matters of science are understood as *strictly separate* perspectives on the same reality,[224] it creates a different kind of modern dualism, something like a god-of-the-gaps[225] conundrum, in which we find God and human agency *outside* (or perhaps, more fairly, *alongside*)[226] the normativity and lawfulness of creation. But from the vantage point of this essay, in which this normativity and lawfulness are to be understood as modes of God's providential control, such a contrast makes little sense. Nevertheless, there are deep resonances between the integration approach he has described and the Reformed and Reformational approach sketched out in this essay—indeed, Jones himself has deep connections to the Reformed tradition and the approach I have outlined may be understood as a particular model of integration. The disparate findings, metaphors, and micro-theories of psychological science find their unity only in the light of the Christian worldview.[227]

---

222. This is similar to if not identical to what Dooyeweerd called "nature-freedom ground motive" or the pre-theoretical vision of reality characteristic of the modern period. See Chaplin, *Herman Dooyeweerd*, 43–44.

223. Jones, "Meaning of Agency and Responsibility."

224. Again, my own view is a kind of levels-of-explanation approach, but one that rejects the modern notion that ultimate-level perspectives can and should be removed from scientific inquiry.

225. Newbigin, *Foolishness to the Greeks*, 66.

226. Jones, "Meaning of Agency and Responsibility," 201.

227. Given the fact that Myers, Powlison, Roberts, and Jones have connections to the Reformed faith, I wonder if a volume on psychology and

Finally, Coe and Hall's helpful and challenging chapter reflects their fascination with pre-modern monastic Christianity. The psychologist, admitting that he cannot wholly separate himself from all tradition, still holds all psychological (and theological) traditions at arm's length, and through spiritual disciplines such as prayer and meditation is transformed into a person of deep faith and upright character, opening them up to reality, creating the possibility for deep insight into psychological truth. This approach, while decidedly anti-modern in some of its tenets, may also perhaps be understood as deeply modern in others. For example, the idea that we need to free ourselves from the blinders of tradition and authority is reminiscent of Enlightenment thinkers.[228] Regardless of its position vis-à-vis modernity, the transformational approach with its keen epistemological insights and willingness to challenge the status-quo, also resonates with some of the deep impulses of a Reformed and Reformational approach. Indeed, this approach may be seen as "transformational" in at least two ways. First, my embrace of the Christian Psychology approach (i.e., recovering the Christian psychology of the past for its ultimate-level theoretical usefulness) will certainly raise the issue of the uniqueness of Christian psychological experience (as my reading of Edwards's *Religious Affections* attests). Second, my hope is that psychological science may be "transformed" as it embraces the truth of the Christian worldview.

Reformed Christianity might be warranted, where different visions of the Reformed faith have an opportunity to dialogue on matters psychological, as iron sharpening iron. My claim to having articulated a "Reformed and Reformational" approach could (and should) be contested. And given the number of institutions desiring to engage psychology from the vantage point of the Reformed faith, such a project might actually have an audience!

228. I need to be careful here—it is possible to find analogies *anywhere* if we look hard enough. But I wonder whether, if Coe and Hall were to revise Kant's classic essay, "What is Enlightenment?" so that it emphasizes the role of the Holy Spirit in the heart of the "scholar" they might not resonate with some of its sentiments, such as the need to be free from tradition and authority, and the motto of the Enlightenment, "Dare to know!," for example. See Kant, "What Is Enlightenment?"

In short, each of the contributions to the two editions of *Psychology & Christianity* can be understood as a way of incarnating a particular variety of Christian commitment in our modern world. Again—given that psychological science still draws its life from the modern worldview, our position vis-à-vis *modernity* remains crucial as we attempt to articulate what a Christian missionary encounter with psychology will look like. In sum, and with inevitable oversimplification, we may summarize the posture[229] toward modernity of our five authors in this way: Myers: *embracing* modernity. Powlison: *contesting* modernity. Roberts and Watson ("step one" and "step two," respectively): *suspending*, then *extending* modernity. Jones: *limiting* modernity. Hall and Coe: *spiritualizing* modernity.[230] From my vantage point, none of these postures toward modernity (and hence psychological science) is entirely satisfactory.

So what sort of response to modernity does this "Reformed and Reformational" essay espouse? I shall turn to that concluding thought in a very brief moment. But first, in view of Coe and Hall's (and *my*) belief that psychology itself and the institutes that teach it ought to be "transformed," we should briefly say something along these lines.

Just what does it take to "transform" the world? Or, more particularly, what would it take to transform psychological science? Interestingly enough, two of the leading contemporary thinkers on this question provide exceedingly humbling responses. To ask if we can change the world, James Davison Hunter says, "is the wrong question."[231] Contrary to the wide-

---

229. See the wonderful discussion of the difference between "postures" and "gestures" in Crouch, *Culture Making*, ch. 5.

230. I have also been playing with Andy Crouch's categories: Myers *consuming* [modern] culture, Powlison *condemning* and/or *critiquing* and/or *copying* culture, Jones *critiquing* culture. Robert and Watson, and Coe and Hall are more difficult to classify using Crouch's categories. But, as a complement to all of the authors, each is in Crouch's term a *creator* of culture. The Reformed and Reformational approach that I advocate vis-à-vis psychological science can celebrate and make good use of these cultural products. See Crouch, *Culture Making*, ch. 4.

231. Hunter, *To Change the World*, 285.

spread belief that "cultures change when people change,"[232] Hunter makes a compelling—and somewhat depressing—case that this is simply not the case. Mainstream cultural change is a heavily contested, "top-down" phenomenon, initiated by certain types of cultural elites in certain types of cultural circumstances.[233] Conservative Christians tend to be on the periphery, with little hope of effecting massive cultural change. Instead of aiming to change the world, Hunter argues, Christians ought to aim to be a "faithful presence within" whatever little corner of the world they inhabit.

In a chapter entitled, "Why We Can't Change the World," Andy Crouch raises some of these same issues. On the widest scale, cultural change is exceedingly difficult to effect, even by the most powerful (he cites the attempt by the United States to create a specific type of cultural change in Iraq as one example). "We can easily deceive ourselves into thinking that changing the world is a great deal easier than it actually is."[234] Still, Crouch gives some insight into how we may forge a faithful Christian presence within psychological science. "Our ability to change culture . . . is a matter of *scale*. On a small enough scale, nearly everyone has the power to change the world."[235] To effect change, he argues, we need to *make something* of the world in which we find ourselves, by creating cultural goods.

In this essay, I have outlined an approach to psychological theory that promises to display the coherence of the Christian worldview and its theoretical relevance to the discipline. In order for this or any other approach to have an effect, we need to *do* and *make* something with them. I believe that Christians in psychology now inhabit a cultural moment in which such activity is possible. Our little corner of the world isn't *that* little—there are well over one hundred CCCU institutions, all of which are dedicated to forging Christ-centered approaches to the academic disciplines, all of which (presumably) have psychology depart-

---

232. Ibid., 16.
233. Ibid., 41–44.
234. Crouch, *Culture Making*, 193.
235. Ibid., 196.

ments, with PhDs on faculty dedicated to the cause. If I may indulge in a wildly unrealistic act of imagination, what would happen if such faculty, trained in secular universities and methods, began to suppose that preparing for and engaging in a missionary encounter with psychological science is their primary scholarly and pedagogical calling?[236] As Hunter argues, God's faithful presence toward us has at least four attributes: he pursues us, he identifies with us, he offers us his life, and he sacrifices for us.[237] Given the freedom that we have within our respective Christian institutions, we can from the safety of such a location pursue psychological science, identify with it, offer it the life of God, and pour out our lives sacrificing for it. We would do so fully realizing that, to the extent that we *as psychologists* foreground our Christian worldview, we will solidify our status as cultural exiles, and that we are likely to be mocked, or, more likely yet, ignored. But inspired by the coherence of our Christian faith, by God's passionate commitment to glorify his own name, and by the evident need within psychological science itself, we may, despite the opposition, attempt to create winsome cultural goods of our own, trusting God with the results.

So what sort of response to modernity *does* this "Reformed and Reformational" essay espouse? Let us tentatively—and with much qualification—try this: *realizing* modernity. This approach ironically "realizes" modernity in the sense that the Christian worldview offers to a repentant psychology the promise of real progress in one of the central goals of the Enlightenment.

The greatest aspiration of modern science, its "Ionian Enchantment," is nothing less than the unification of knowledge. This enchantment, as E. O. Wilson explains, is named after the first of the pre-Socratics (at least according to the textbooks), the father of Greek philosophy, Thales of Miletus, Ionia. Thales famously sought to unify knowledge by arguing that all material reality ultimately reduces to water. Though his solution is now universally rejected, his quest, to find the key that unlocks all knowledge *immanently*, in the creation itself, continues to this

---

236. See Goheen and Bartholomew, *Living at the Crossroads*, 8–9.
237. Hunter, *To Change the World*, 241–43.

day. This quest, rightly characterized by Wilson as religious, is, for reasons discussed above, an Icarus-like wax-winged flight toward the sun, foredoomed to failure.[238] The creation, in all of its magnificent and complex interrelatedness, cannot in the final analysis explain itself.

If I may revise Tertullian, only in Jerusalem can the Ionian Enchantment be requited. Laplace fundamentally misrepresented the reality that he had through mathematics described when, speaking of God, famously boasted, "I have no need of that hypothesis."[239] The Triune God is no hypothesis. He is the purpose and precondition of all that is, the one for whom and through whom all things exist, the one in whom all things cohere.

Psychology need not repent[240] of its sophisticated methods, or its careful attentiveness to empirical reality, or its hard-won scientific and theoretical accomplishments. But it does need to repent of its marginalization of the One who ultimately gave it the marvelous *psyche* to study, the desire and ability to study it, and the Word that provides light for this path of inquiry. As it does, psychology will finally be in position to forge the unification that it has long sought.[241] The question implied in the

---

238. Wilson, who argues that "all tangible phenomena . . . are ultimately reducible to . . . the laws of physics," claims that the daring of Icarus was not hubris but rather "a saving human grace" (Wilson, *Consilience*, 4–7, 266). For a sketch of *why* such a quest is foredoomed to failure, see the discussion on the modes of God's providential control. For a fuller discussion, see also Chaplin, *Herman Dooyeweerd*, ch. 4.

239. He *was* likely right to reject the hypothesis of a deity who needs to *intervene* in the solar system "for frequent adjustment and repair" (Peters, "Protestantism and the Sciences," 312). Laplace really did have no need of *that* hypothesis, which was a good thing—it signaled the advance of scientific theory. This again suggests the problems with relegating divine action to "intervention." Laplace's famous phrase misrepresents reality when it is used to imply that science can give a satisfactory accounting of the world apart from the One whose providential control of the universe extends even to its laws and norms.

240. I struggled over whether to use this word but decided to keep it, given that the issues at stake are ultimately religious.

241. See note 86.

title *Psychology & Christianity*, therefore, is not an esoteric debate for those with concerns peripheral to the mainstream. The admittedly "astonishing hypothesis" sketched out in this essay is that our answer to the question of the relation between Christian faith and psychological science may actually contain the answer to the most profound and elusive question of the discipline.

God has revealed himself in two books. These books are meant to be read *together*, and exegeted with the utmost care. As we do this, we shall move closer to Jonathan Edwards's youthful dream "To shew how all arts and sciences, the more they are perfected, the more they issue in divinity, and coincide with it, and appear to be parts of it."[242] One way to be faithfully present within our little and insignificant corner of the world of psychological science is to try to show again and again the unity of the two books, that all *psychological* things do indeed cohere in Christ, that the theoretical unity long longed for in psychology is to be found *inside* the wide rationality of the Christian

---

242. Edwards, "Outline of 'A Rational Account,'" 397. For an estimate of when Edwards wrote this (i.e., in his mid- to late-twenties) see Marsden, *Jonathan Edwards*, 482. I was, initially at least, disappointed to find, after having written this final paragraph, that Eric Johnson, the editor of *Psychology & Christianity: Five Views* beat me to the punch in choosing this as his closing quote. Whether this is a case of cryptomnesia (I had not to my knowledge read any of Johnson's closing chapter until after writing this essay) or simply deep compatibility of vision, I am not sure. Perhaps it is both. But the Edwards quote, which I have long loved, is apt, so I decided to retain it. See Johnson, "Gaining Understanding," 311. Incidentally, I did finally get around to reading Johnson's conclusion. It is a lovely piece dealing with how we ought to approach the diversity of opinions expressed in *Five Views*. I fully affirm his suggestion that "this book's vigorous debate points to a larger reality that lies behind all of the views, and this reality requires listening to all of them and appropriating the valid insights of each one, in order to get 'the biggest picture' we can." (Johnson, "Getting Understanding," 29). Although I don't know how Johnson would feel about my claim that a specifically Reformed and Reformational metasystem can make a helpful contribution to this big picture (though he clearly has at the very least been strongly influenced by the Reformed tradition), I trust that this essay generally strikes the kind of tone he suggests and have inserted a few footnotes to that effect.

worldview.[243] David Powlison is right—we have much work to do.

Bibliography

Ames, William. *The Marrow of Theology*. Translated by John Dykstra Eusden. Original edition, 1624. Grand Rapids: Baker, 1968.

———. *Technometry*. Translated by Lee W. Gibbs. Philadelphia: University of Pennsylvania Press, 1979.

Aronson, Elliot. "The Return of the Repressed: Dissonance Theory Makes a Comeback." *Psychological Inquiry* 3 (1992) 303–11.

Bahnsen, Greg L. *Van Til's Apologetic: Readings and Analysis*. Phillipsburg, NJ: Presbyterian & Reformed, 1998.

Baumeister, Roy F. "Religion and Psychology: Introduction to the Special Issue." *Psychological Inquiry* 13 (2002) 165–67.

Baumeister, Roy F., and Mark R. Leary. "The Need to Belong: Desire for Interpersonal Attachments as a Fundamental Human Motivation." *Psychological Bulletin* 10 (1995) 497–529.

Baumeister, Roy F., and Dianne M. Tice. "Rethinking and Reclaiming the Interdisciplinary Role of Personality

---

243. As Newbigin said, "the conflict between the two views will not be [ultimately] settled on the basis of logical argument. The view will prevail that is seen to offer—both in theory and in practice—the widest rationality, the greatest capacity to give meaning to the whole of experience. This is as much a matter of faithful endeavor and costly obedience [i.e., faithful presence?] as of clarity and coherence of argument." As is the case in "every true missionary encounter," this is nothing less than a call to a "radical conversion," to "a 'paradigm shift' that leads to a new vision of how things are and, not at once but gradually, to the development of a new plausibility structure in which the most real of all realities is the living God" (Newbigin, *Foolishness to the Greeks*, 64).

Psychology: The Science of Human Nature Should Be the Center of the Social Sciences and Humanities." *Journal of Research in Personality* 30 (1996) 363–73.

Behe, Michael J. *The Edge of Evolution: The Search for the Limits of Darwinism.* New York: Free Press, 2007.

Benjamin, Ludy T. *A Brief History of Modern Psychology.* Malden, MA: Blackwell, 2007.

Bloom, Paul. *How Pleasure Works: The New Science of Why We Like What We Like.* New York: Norton, 2010.

Bozeman, Theodore Dwight. *Protestants in an Age of Science.* Chapel Hill, NC: University of North Carolina Press, 1977.

Browne, Janet. *Darwin's Origin of Species: A Biography.* New York: Grove, 2006.

Buckner, Noel, and Robert Whittlesey. "Why Sex?" In *Evolution.* no pages. DVD. Boston: WGBH, 2001.

Buss, David M. "Evolutionary Psychology: A New Paradigm for Psychological Science." *Psychological Inquiry* 6 (1995) 1–30.

Calvin, John. *The Institutes of the Christian Religion.* Translated by Ford Lewis Battles. Edited by John T. McNeill. Louisville: Westminster John Knox, 1960.

Chaplin, Jonathan. *Herman Dooyeweerd: Christian Philosopher of State and Civil Society.* Notre Dame: University of Notre Dame Press, 2011.

Clouser, Roy A. *The Myth of Religious Neutrality: An Essay on the Hidden Role of Religious Belief in Theories.* Notre Dame: University of Notre Dame Press, 2005.

Coe, John. "The Call and Task of This Journal." *Journal of Spiritual Formation and Soul Care* 1 (2008) 2–4.

Coe, John H., and Todd W. Hall. "A Transformational Psychology View." In Johnson, ed., *Psychology & Christianity: Five Views*, 199–226.

Collins, Gary R. "An Integration View." In Johnson and Stanton, eds., *Psychology & Christianity: Four Views*, 102–29.

Coyne, Jerry A. *Why Evolution Is True*. New York: Viking, 2009.

Crouch, Andy. *Culture Making: Recovering Our Creative Calling*. Downers Grove, IL: InterVarsity, 2008.

Currid, John D. *A Study Commentary on Genesis*. Webster, NY: Evangelical Press, 2003.

Danziger, Kurt. *Constructing the Subject: Historical Origins of Psychological Research*. New York: Cambridge University Press, 1990.

Darwin, Charles. *The Origin of Species*. New York: Bantam, 1859.

Dawkins, Richard. *The God Delusion*. New York: Houghton Mifflin, 2006.

———. *The Greatest Show on Earth: The Evidence for Evolution*. New York: Free Press, 2009.

Ecklund, Elaine Howard. *Science vs. Religion: What Scientists Really Think*. New York: Oxford University Press, 2010.

Edwards, Jonathan. "Outline of 'A Rational Account.'" In *Works of Jonathan Edwards*. Vol. 6, *Scientific and Philosophical Writings*, 396–97. New Haven: Yale University Press, 1980.

———. "Two Dissertations." In *Works of Jonathan Edwards*, Vol. 8, *Ethical Writings*, 399–627. New Haven: Yale University Press, 1989.

Evans, C. Stephen. "Christian Perspectives on the Sciences of Man." *Christian Scholar's Review* 6 (1976) 97–113.

———. *Preserving the Person: A Look at the Human Sciences.* Grand Rapids: Baker, 1977.

Festinger, Leon, and James M. Carlsmith. "Cognitive Consequences of Forced Compliance." *Journal of Abnormal and Social Psychology* 58 (1959) 203–10.

Fiering, Norman. *Moral Philosophy at Seventeenth-Century Harvard: A Discipline in Transition.* Chapel Hill, NC: University of North Carolina Press, 1981.

Frame, John M. *The Doctrine of God.* Phillipsburg, NJ: Presbyterian & Reformed, 2002.

———. *The Doctrine of the Knowledge of God.* Phillipsburg, NJ: Presbyterian & Reformed, 1987.

Gaulin, Steven J. C., and Donald H. McBurney. *Evolutionary Psychology.* Upper Saddle River, NJ: Pearson Prentice Hall, 2004.

George, Timothy. *Theology of the Reformers.* Nashville: Broadman & Holman, 1988.

Gerrig, Richard J., Philip G. Zimbardo, Serge Desmarais, and Tammy Ivanco. *Psychology and Life.* Toronto: Pearson Education Canada, 2009.

Gleitman, Henry, Daniel Reisberg, and James Gross. *Psychology.* New York: Norton, 2007.

Goethals, George R. "Dissonance and Self-Justification." *Psychological Inquiry* 3 (1992) 327–29.

Goheen, Michael W., and Craig G. Bartholomew. *Living at the Crossroads: An Introduction to Christian Worldview.* Grand Rapids: Baker Academic, 2008.

González, Justo L. *The Story of Christianity*. 2 vols. New York: HarperCollins, 1985.

Goodwin, C. James. *Research in Psychology: Methods and Design*. Hoboken, NJ: John Wiley & Sons, 2005.

Gray, Peter. *Psychology*. New York: Worth, 2011.

Harmon-Jones, Eddie, and Judson Mills. "An Introduction to Cognitive Dissonance Theory and an Overview of Current Perspectives on the Theory." In *Cognitive Dissonance: Progress on a Pivotal Theory in Social Psychology*, 3–21. Washington, DC: American Psychological Association, 1999.

Harrison, Peter. *The Fall of Man and the Foundations of Science*. New York: Cambridge University Press, 2009.

Hooykaas, R. *Religion and the Rise of Modern Science*. Vancouver, BC: Regent College Publishing, 1972.

Hunter, James Davison. *To Change the World: The Irony, Tragedy, and Possibility of Christianity in the Late Modern World*. New York: Oxford University Press, 2010.

Johnson, Eric L. "Gaining Understanding through Five Views." In Johnson, ed., *Psychology & Christianity: Five Views*, 292–313.

———, ed. *Psychology & Christianity, Five Views*. Downers Grove, IL: IVP Academic, 2010.

Johnson, Eric L. and Stanton L. Jones, eds. *Psychology & Christianity: Four Views*. Downers Grove, IL: InterVarsity, 2000.

Johnston, Charles M. *McMaster University*. Toronto: University of Toronto Press, 1981.

Jones, Stanton L. "An Integration View." In Johnson, ed., *Psychology & Christianity: Five Views*, 101–28.

———. "The Meaning of Agency and Responsibility in Light of Social Science Research." In *Limning the Psyche: Explorations in Christian Psychology*, 186–205. Eugene, OR: Wipf & Stock, 1997.

Kant, Immanuel. "What Is Enlightenment?" In *The Enlightenment: A Brief History with Documents*, by Margaret C. Jacob, 202–7. Bedford Series in History and Culture. Boston: Bedford/St. Martins, 2001.

Keltner, Dacher. *Born to Be Good: The Science of a Meaningful Life*. New York: Norton, 2009.

Kosits, Russell D. "Redeeming Psychology Means Developing an Apologetic Edge." *Comment*, June 2009, 40–42. Online: http://www.cardus.ca/comment/article/1047/

———. "What Would It Mean to Redeem Psychology?" *Comment*, June 2009, 18–22.
Online: http://www.cardus.ca/comment/article/1040/

Kuhn, Thomas S. *The Structure of Scientific Revolutions*. Chicago: University of Chicago Press, 1996.

Kuklick, Bruce. "On Critical History." In *Religious Advocacy and American History*. Edited by Bruce Kuklick, 54–64. Grand Rapids: Eerdmans, 1997.

Lane, Timothy S., and Paul David Tripp. *How People Change*. Greensboro, NC: New Growth Press, 2008.

Leary, David E. "Psyche's Muse: The Role of Metaphor in the History of Psychology." In *Metaphors in the History of Psychology*, 1–78. New York: Cambridge University Press, 1990.

Letham, Robert. *The Holy Trinity: In Scripture, History, Theology, and Worship*. Phillipsburg, NJ: P & R, 2004.

Levitin, Daniel J. *This Is Your Brain on Music*. New York: Plume, 2006.

Marsden, George M. *Jonathan Edwards: A Life*. New Haven: Yale University Press, 2003.

———. *The Outrageous Idea of Christian Scholarship*. New York: Oxford University Press, 1997.

———. *The Soul of the American University: From Protestant Establishment to Established Nonbelief*. New York: Oxford University Press, 1994.

———. *Understanding Fundamentalism and Evangelicalism*. Grand Rapids: Eerdmans, 1991.

McGrath, Alister. *A Fine-tuned Universe: The Quest for God in Science and Theology*. Louisville: Westminster John Knox, 2009.

———. *The Open Secret: A New Vision for Natural Theology*. Malden, MA: Blackwell, 2008.

———. *Reformation Thought: An Introduction*. Cambridge, MA: Blackwell, 1993.

Miller, Geoffrey. *The Mating Mind: How Sexual Choice Shaped the Evolution of Human Nature*. New York: Anchor, 2000.

Miller, Perry. *The New England Mind: The Seventeenth Century*. Cambridge, MA: Belknap, 1939.

Myers, David G. *A Friendly Letter to Skeptics and Atheists: Musings on Why God Is Good and Faith Isn't Evil*. San Francisco: Jossey-Bass, 2008.

———. *The Human Puzzle: Psychological Research and Christian Belief*. New York: Harper & Row, 1978.

———. "A Levels-of-Explanation View." In Johnson and Stanton, eds., *Psychology & Christianity: Four Views*, 54–83.

———. *Psychology*. 9th ed. New York: Worth, 2010.

———. "Redeeming Psychology Means Taking Psychological Science Seriously." *Comment*, June 2009, 23–25. Online: http://www.cardus.ca/comment/article/1041

Myers, David G., and Malcom A. Jeeves. *Psychology through the Eyes of Faith*. New York: HarperCollins, 2003.

Newbigin, Lesslie. *Foolishness to the Greeks: The Gospel and Western Culture*. Grand Rapids: Eerdmans, 1986.

Peters, Ted. "Protestantism and the Sciences." In *The Blackwell Companion to Protestantism*. Edited by Alister E. McGrath and Darren C. Marks, 306–21. Malden, MA: Blackwell, 2004.

Pinker, Steven. *The Language Instinct*. New York: HarperCollins, 1994.

Plantinga, Alvin. *Where the Conflict Really Lies: Science, Religion, and Naturalism*. New York: Oxford University Press, 2011.

Powlison, David. "A Biblical Counseling View." In Johnson and Stanton, eds., *Psychology & Christianity: Four Views*, 196–225.

———. "A Biblical Counseling View." In Johnson, ed., *Psychology & Christianity: Five Views*, 245–73.

———. "Do You See?" *The Journal of Biblical Counseling* 11 (1993) 3–4.

———. "Redeeming Psychology Means Learning How to Better Use the Bible in Psychological Work." *Comment*, June 2009, 34–36. Online: http://www.cardus.ca/comment/article/1045.

Poythress, Vern S. *Symphonic Theology: The Validity of Multiple Perspectives in Theology*. Phillipsburg, NJ: P & R, 1987.

Rauch, Frederick A. *Psychology: Or, a View of the Human Soul*. New York: M. W. Dodd, 1840.

Roberts, Robert C. "A Christian Psychology View." In Johnson and Stanton, eds., *Psychology and Christianity: Four Views*, 148–77.

———. "Redeeming Psychology Means Recovering the Christian Psychology of the Past." *Comment*, June 2009, 37–39. Online: http://www.cardus.ca/comment/article/1046.

———. *Spiritual Emotions: A Psychology of Christian Virtues*. Grand Rapids: Eerdmans, 2007.

Roberts, Robert C., and P. J. Watson. "A Christian Psychology View." In Johnson, ed., *Psychology & Christianity: Five Views*, 149–78.

Rupp, E. Gordon, and Philip S. Watson, eds. *Luther and Erasmus: Free Will and Salvation*. Philadelphia: Westminster, 1969.

Scott-Phillips, Thomas C., Thomas E. Dickins, and Stuart A. West. "Evolutionary Theory and the Ultimate-Proximate Distinction in the Human Behavioral Sciences." *Perspectives on Psychological Science* 6 (2011) 38–47.

Sheldon, Kennon M. *Optimal Human Being: An Integrated Multi-Level Perspective*. Mahwah, NJ: Lawrence Erlbaum Associates, 2004.

Sternberg, Robert J., ed. *Unity in Psychology: Possibility or Pipedream?* Washington, DC: American Psychological Association, 2005.

Stevenson, Daryl H., Brian E. Eck, and Peter C. Hill, eds. *Psychology and Christianity Integration: Seminal Works That Shaped the Movement*. Batavia, IL: Christian Association for Psychological Studies, 2007.

Storr, Anthony. *Freud: A Very Short Introduction*. New York: Oxford University Press, 1989.

Tavris, Carol, and Elliot Aronson. *Mistakes Were Made (but Not by Me): Why We Justify Foolish Beliefs, Bad Decisions, and Hurtful Acts*. Orlando, FL: Harcourt, 2007.

Teske, Roland. "Augustine's Philosophy of Memory." In *The Cambridge Companion to Augustine*, 148–58. New York: Cambridge University Press, 2001.

Van Til, Cornelius. "Nature and Scripture." In *The Infallible Word*, 263–301. Phillipsburg, NJ: P & R, 1967.

Watson, P. J. "Whose Psychology? Which Rationality? Christian Psychology within an Ideological Surround after Postmodernism." *Journal of Psychology and Christianity* 30 (2011) 307–16.

Welch, Edward T. "Who Are We? Needs, Longings, and the Image of God in Man." *The Journal of Biblical Counseling* 13 (1994) 25–38.

Wilson, Edward O. *Consilience: The Unity of Knowledge*. New York: Alfred A. Knopf, 1998.

Wolterstorff, Nicholas. *Reason within the Bounds of Religion*. Grand Rapids: Eerdmans, 1984.

Book Reviews in the Online Version of MJTM Vol. 13

http://www.mcmaster.ca/mjtm/volume13.htm

Allison, Gregg R. *Historical Theology: An Introduction to Christian Doctrine.* Grand Rapids: Zondervan, 2011. Reviewed by David Corey.

Arnold, Clinton E. *Ephesians.* Grand Rapids: Zondervan, 2010. Reviewed by Jonathan D. Numada.

Bowen, John, ed. *The Missionary Letters of Vincent Donovan: 1957–1973.* Eugene, OR: Pickwick, 2011. Reviewed by Lee Beach.

Branson, Mark Lau, and Juan F. Martínez. *Churches, Cultures and Leadership: A Practical Theology of Congregations and Ethnicities.* Downers Grove, IL: IVP Academic, 2011. Reviewed by Kevin Book-Satterlee.

Burnett, Amy Nelson, ed. *John Calvin, Myth and Reality: Images and Impact of Geneva's Reformer. Papers of the 2009 Calvin Studies Society Colloquium.* Eugene, OR: Cascade, 2011. Reviewed by John Schuit.

deSilva, David A. *Sacramental Life: Spiritual Formation through the Book of Common Prayer.* Downers Grove, IL: InterVarsity, 2008. Reviewed by Matthew Dowling.

Deweese, Garrett J. *Doing Philosophy as a Christian.* Downers Grove, IL: InterVarsity, 2011. Reviewed by Timothy D. Sasaki.

Dickson, John. *Humilitas: A Lost Key to Life, Love, and Leadership.* Grand Rapids: Zondervan, 2011. Reviewed by Lois Dow.

Douglas, J. D., Merrill C. Tenney, and Moises Silva. *Zondervan Illustrated Bible Dictionary.* Grand Rapids: Zondervan, 2011. Reviewed by Ingrid Reichard.

Galli, Mark. *Chaos and Grace: Discovering the Liberating Work of the Holy Spirit.* Grand Rapids: Baker, 2011. Reviewed by Bradley K. Broadhead.

Hamilton, James M. *God's Glory in Salvation through Judgment: A Biblical Theology.* Wheaton: Crossway, 2010. Reviewed by Celucien L. Joseph.

Heath, Gordon, and Paul Wilson, eds. *Baptists in Public Life in Canada.* McMaster General Studies. Eugene, OR: Pickwick, 2012.

Horton, Michael S. *For Calvinism.* Grand Rapids: Zondervan, 2011. Reviewed by Gene Haas.

Horton, Michael S. *The Christian Faith: A Systematic Theology for Pilgrims on the Way.* Grand Rapids: Zondervan, 2011. Reviewed by J. Clare Fuller.

Houston, James M. and Michael Parker. *A Vision for the Aging Church: Renewing Ministry for and by Seniors.* Downers Grove, IL: IVP Academic, 2011. Reviewed by Dorothy Hunse.

Jobes, Karen H. *Letters to the Church: A Survey of Hebrews and the General Epistles.* Grand Rapids: Zondervan, 2011. Reviewed by Matthew Forrest Lowe.

Köstenberger, Andreas J. *A Theology of John's Gospel and Letters: The Word, the Christ, the Son of God.* Grand Rapids: Zondervan, 2009. Reviewed by Rocky Fong.

Reviews

McDowell, Sean, and Jonathan Morrow, eds. *Is God Just a Human Invention? And Seventeen Other Questions Raised by the New Atheists*. Grand Rapids: Kregel, 2010. Reviewed by Bruce Worthington.

Mead, James K. *Biblical Theology: Issues, Methods and Themes*. Louisville: Westminster John Knox, 2007. Reviewed by Stephen Dempster.

Moyise, Steve. *Jesus and Scripture: Studying the New Testament Use of the Old Testament*. Grand Rapids: Baker Academic, 2011. Reviewed by Deven K. MacDonald.

Naselli, Andrew David, and Collin Hansen. *Four Views on the Spectrum of Evangelicalism*. Grand Rapids: Zondervan, 2011. Reviewed by Gordon L. Heath.

Ockholm, Trevecca. *Kingdom Family: Re-envisioning God's Plan for Marriage and Family*. Eugene, OR: Cascade, 2012. Reviewed by Kelvin F. Mutter.

Olson, Roger E. *Against Calvinism*. Grand Rapids: Zondervan, 2011. Reviewed by Gene Haas.

Peterson, James. C. *Changing Human Nature: Ecology, Ethics, Genes and God*. Grand Rapids: Eerdmans, 2010. Reviewed by Francesco Anello.

Plummer, Robert L. ed. *Journeys of Faith: Evangelicalism, Eastern Orthodoxy, Catholicism, and Anglicanism*. Grand Rapids: Zondervan, 2012. Reviewed by Michael P. Knowles.

Powlinson, David. *The Biblical Counseling Movement: History and Context*. Greensboro, NC: New Growth Press, 2010. Reviewed by Kelvin F. Mutter.

Quicke, Michael J. *Preaching as Worship: An Integrative Approach to Formation in Your Church*. Grand Rapids: Baker, 2011. Reviewed by Michael P. Knowles.

Schreiner, Thomas R. *Galatians*. Grand Rapids: Zondervan, 2010. Reviewed by Bryan R. Dyer.

Scorgie, Glen G. et al., eds. *Dictionary of Christian Spirituality*. Grand Rapids: Zondervan, 2011. Reviewed by Michael P. Knowles.

Swindoll, Charles R. *Insights on Revelation*. Grand Rapids: Zondervan, 2011. Reviewed by Dan Morrison.

Tucker, Ruth A. *Parade of Faith: A Biographical History of the Christian Church*. Grand Rapids: Zondervan, 2011. Reviewed by Gordon L. Heath.

Volf, Miroslav. *A Public Faith: How Followers of Christ Should Serve the Common Good*. Grand Rapids: Brazos, 2011. Reviewed by Kelvin F. Mutter.

Weeks, Stuart. *Ecclesiastes and Scepticism*. New York: T. & T. Clark, 2012. Reviewed by Russell L. Meek.

Williams, Michael. *How to Read the Bible through the Jesus Lens: A Guide to Christ-Focused Reading of Scripture*. Grand Rapids: Zondervan, 2012. Reviewed by Laura Thompson.

Witherington, Ben III. *Is There a Doctor in the House? An Insider's Story and Advice on Becoming a Bible Scholar*. Grand Rapids: Zondervan, 2011. Reviewed by Lois Dow.

www.ingramcontent.com/pod-product-compliance
Lightning Source LLC
Chambersburg PA
CBHW051743230426
43670CB00012B/2134